THE
TOP 100
HEALTHY RECIPES
FOR BABIES & TODDLERS

THE
TOP 100
HEALTHY RECIPES
FOR BABIES & TODDLERS

Renée Elliott

DELICIOUS, HEALTHY RECIPES FOR PURÉES, FINGER FOODS AND MEALS

DUNCAN BAIRD PUBLISHERS

LONDON

The Top 100 Healthy Recipes
For Babies & Toddlers
Renée Elliott

This edition first published in the United Kingdom and
Ireland in 2013 by Duncan Baird Publishers, an imprint of
Watkins Publishing Limited
Sixth Floor
75 Wells Street
London W1T 3QH

A member of Osprey Group

Managing Editor: Grace Cheetham
Editors: Nicole Bator, Krissy Mallett, Victoria Fernandez
Salom
Managing Designer: Manisha Patel
Designer: Sailesh Patel
Commissioned photography: Simon Smith
Food Stylist: Mari Mererid Williams
Prop Stylist: Wei Tang

A CIP record for this book is available from the British Library

ISBN: 978-1-84899-107-1
10 9 8 7 6 5 4 3 2 1

Typeset in News Gothic
Colour reproduction by PDQ, UK
Printed in China

Publisher's Note
The information in this book is not intended as a substitute
for professional medical advice and treatment. If you are
pregnant or breastfeeding or have any special dietary
requirements or medical conditions, it is recommended
that you consult a medical professional before following
any of the information or recipes contained in this book.
Watkins Publishing Limited, or any other persons who
ɔn this publication,
any errors or omissions,
found in the recipes or
nay arise as a result of
ɪr following the advice

ıit and vegetables
herbs
measurements
1 cup = 250ml

ɛn small amounts of an
mbol for sesame oil. Dairy
ɔow's, goat's or sheep's milk.
ɪo recipes using cheese;
please check the manufacturer's labelling before purchase
to ensure cheeses are vegetarian. Ensure that only the
relevantly identified foods are given to anyone with
a food allergy or intolerance.

Acknowledgments
Huge thanks, hugs and kisses to my husband Brian
and my kids for eating my food and being so patient;
my mom for her recipes; Julia for her total support;
Nathalie for caring for my children; Allison for helping out
without being asked; Veronica for her encouragement;
Molly for tuna pie and prawn bake; and Maggie for the knife.
Thank you to Borra, Grace, Luana and Nicole; without you
there simply wouldn't be a book. And to Suzannah Olivier,
whose book *What Should I Feed My Baby?* inspired me
when I was a new mother.

CONTENTS

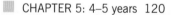

KEY TO SYMBOLS

VEGETARIAN:
Contains no meat, poultry, game, fish, shellfish or animal by-products.

WHEAT-FREE:
Contains no wheat, wheat flour or wheat products.

GLUTEN-FREE:
Contains no gluten-based grains or products, including wheat, barley, rye, oats, spelt and Kamut.

DAIRY-FREE:
Contains no dairy products, including milk, cheese, yogurt, kefir or butter.

EGG-FREE:
Contains no eggs or egg products.

NUT-FREE:
Contains no nuts (almonds, Brazil nuts, cashew nuts, chestnuts, coconut, hazelnuts, macadamia nuts, peanuts, pecans, pine nuts, pistachio nuts and walnuts) or nut oils.

SEED-FREE:
Contains no seeds (flax, hemp, pumpkin, sesame and sunflower) or seed oils.

INTRODUCTION

Some people worry about giving their child a good education or getting him to excel at sports or a musical instrument, but for me the most important thing is health. You could have the brightest, most gifted, most well-educated child, but without good health, he won't go far. With good health he can achieve his dreams and fulfil his potential. And it's easier to be happy when you're healthy.

WHY IS HEALTH SO IMPORTANT?

When I talk about health, I'm not just talking about your child being well today or when he's a teenager. I'm talking about creating health and healthy habits to last a lifetime. You can eat bad food for years and feel okay – but you could slowly be creating unease in your body that becomes disease as you age. Other factors like polluted air, chemically treated water, and of course, stress can all take their toll on the body; but while you can't do that much about those things, you can control what your family eats. What you put in their mouths are the ingredients that their bodies use to grow, nurture and repair themselves. Before you start cooking, it's important to think about the ingredients you give your body every day.

GOOD FOOD VS. BAD FOOD

The bad-food category includes highly processed, refined products such as store-bought cakes, breads, doughnuts, sausages, fast food, fizzy drinks and sweets. Basic ingredients to avoid are hydrogenated fats, monosodium glutamate (MSG), and artificial flavourings, colourings, additives and preservatives. Hydrogenated fats are laden with highly processed trans fats that the body cannot process. They're used because they're cheap, easy to work with and extend a food's shelf life. Artificial preservatives make bad, cheap food last longer than it should, and artificial flavours, colours and additives make it look and taste better than it should. A chocolate chip cookie made with hydrogenated fat and artificial ingredients can sit on the supermarket shelf for months, losing what little nutritional value it has as it ages. The same cookie made with butter and natural ingredients will go out of date more quickly because its ingredients are perishable, but who wants to eat old food?

Good food comes directly from nature: fruit, vegetables, grains, nuts, seeds, dairy, fish and meat. It does not contain chemicals or lots of additives. Good food is organic food. Organic products don't depend on chemical fertilizers, pesticides, additives or genetically modified ingredients, which are poisons that stay on our food, go into our water and are pretty much everywhere on the planet now. If you want the best-quality food, buy organic. It's that simple. Research funded by the European Union shows that organic food contains higher levels of some nutrients, including vitamin C; essential minerals, such as calcium, magnesium and iron; cancer-fighting antioxidants; and omega-3 fats. If organic meat doesn't suit your budget, buy a little when you can and then provide protein through seeds, nuts, grains, beans, tempeh, yogurt, cheese, eggs and fish instead. Remember that variety is always the best policy anyway, and eating less meat is better not only for human health but for the health of our environment.

GETTING STARTED

Now that you understand why good, natural, organic food is so important, it's time to get started. The recipes in this book are easy, provide your baby with the best possible nutrition and taste great. Whether it's the food or the utensils you're using, make sure that everything you cook with is healthy for your child.

INGREDIENTS

Whole Grains: A grain is whole when it contains the bran, germ and endosperm. The bran and germ of the grain are rich in fibre, vitamins, minerals, antioxidants and healthy fats. The endosperm is high in simple carbohydrates and low in nutrients. When grain is refined, the bran and germ are removed, leaving just the endosperm. The body quickly breaks down the endosperm's simple sugars and releases them into the bloodstream. This is one reason why eating refined grains and refined grain products, such as white flour, white bread, white rice and white pasta, has such a harsh effect on blood sugar levels and energy. With whole grains, you know all the goodness is still inside. Whole grains add richness and variety to your diet. They can help lower the risk of type 2 diabetes and have been shown to protect against childhood asthma. Most people eat wheat regularly, and perhaps some rye, but it's important to rotate these with other whole grains, such as amaranth, barley, buckwheat, brown rices (black, jasmine, red Camargue and wild), corn, Kamut, millet, oats, quinoa, rye and spelt.

Wholemeal Spelt Flour: Use wholemeal spelt flour to make baked treats and snacks nutritious. You can easily change your existing recipes to use wholemeal, preferably spelt, flour. For breads and cookies, I use 100%; for cupcakes, I use a 50/50 mixture of wholemeal and white spelt flours for a lighter texture. Spelt, a relative of wheat, is an ancient grain that, unlike wheat, has not been hybridized and manipulated over the years in order to make it easier to harvest and use.

Healthy Fats: It's important to realize that not all fat is bad. Good fats are monounsaturated and polyunsaturated fats, which include essential fatty acids that are vital to our diet, especially during childhood. They reduce the risk of cancer, heart disease, allergies, arthritis, eczema, depression, fatigue, infections and more. Good fats include olive oil, flaxseed oil, hemp seed oil, oily fish oils, nuts and seeds. Yogurt, which isn't very high in fat, is another great choice, so buy full-fat natural yogurt for your baby. I like to cook with butter because it's a good high-heat, natural fat. Avoid hydrogenated fats, including margarines that are made of hydrogenated or partially hydrogenated fats. If you want to use margarines, choose organic ones which are made with non-hydrogenated oils.

Cow's Milk Alternatives: Cow's milk can cause health problems for children and adults. Because we don't need milk after weaning, we begin to lose the ability to produce our own enzymes to digest it; as we get older, milk becomes more difficult to digest. Furthermore, cow's milk is pasteurized, which means that all the enzymes in it that help us to digest it have been killed. Cultured milk products, such as yogurt and cheese, are fermented, making them healthier and easier to digest. Yogurt is great because it contains live bifidus and acidophilus cultures, which are the good bacteria that should inhabit the gut. They keep harmful bacteria under control, ensure that the body produces vitamins and enzymes and keep down the level of toxins in the body, preventing potential diseases. Kefir contains those live cultures, plus healthy yeast cultures, which help restore a better balance to the gut flora, so it's even better. Wherever feasible, opt for products made from goat's and sheep's milk, which have smaller fat globules and are more easily digested than cow's milk. Milk substitutes, such as oat milk, rice milk or soya milk, are good for breakfast cereals, but use soya milk and rice milk in moderation. Soya contains isoflavones, or hormone (oestrogen) mimics, which can disrupt a baby's normal hormone balance. Rice milk contains low levels of arsenic, so children from one to five years should not have too much of it. Once a baby has weaned, he can drink water. Give your child water to drink and let him get calcium from food.

Natural Sugars: White and brown sugar, glucose, molasses, honey and maple syrup are all simple sugars. Concentrated simple sugar hits the bloodstream quickly and causes a rapid increase in blood sugar levels. This gives you an energy surge followed by a quick drop as the body rushes to rebalance. Diabetes is the extreme form of blood sugar imbalance and has become more common in children. Furthermore, sugar that is not used by the body is converted into fat. But you can mould your baby's tastes. He doesn't know about sweetened yogurt, so serve natural. Refrain from sweetening sour fruits, such as raspberries, and let him experience their natural flavour. Fruit contains fructose, a simple sugar, but to metabolize it the body must first convert fructose into glucose, which means that it releases slowly. So even though fruits contain simple sugars, they are, in general, much better than other sugars when you eat the whole fruit. A special word about honey: do not give honey to babies younger than one year because it carries a slight risk of botulism. The best sweetener is brown rice syrup, which is made up mostly of complex sugars and, therefore, releases more slowly into the bloodstream. To convert the sugar in your recipes to brown rice syrup, use 310ml/10¾fl oz/ 1¼ cups brown rice syrup for every 220g/7¾oz/1 cup sugar and reduce liquids by 60ml/ 2fl oz/¼ cup. Beware of 'sugar-free' foods as they often include artificial sweeteners, such as saccharin, aspartame and sorbitol – all of which have been linked to health problems.

Reduced Salt: All foods naturally contain sodium, which our bodies need. Eating too much added salt, however, is linked to all sorts of diseases, and children's kidneys struggle if made to deal with added salt. Your child's palate is pure, so help shape it by making food without added salt. Wait until after one year to introduce salt and then use it only very sparingly. To satisfy a salt craving in an older child, offer toasted seaweed, like nori, as a snack.

UTENSILS

Non-Toxic Storage Containers: Plastic contains harmful chemicals, including phthalates. Studies by Greenpeace show that some of these chemicals may interfere with the hormone systems that regulate normal growth and reproductive development in children. Plastics are difficult to recycle, too. They either sit in landfills or are burned, often emitting dioxins and heavy metals. Instead, store and serve food in metal containers with plastic lids that don't come into contact with the food. Other good alternatives to plastic are glass or ceramic. If you do use plastic, always let the food you're storing cool completely before you put it in a plastic container, to reduce the risk of anything harmful leaching into the food.

Stainless Steel Cookware: Good stainless steel cookware is ideal for everyday use. It can be heated to a high temperature, you can use any utensils with it and it lasts a long time. Non-stick cookware has its conveniences, but it's better to avoid it as much as possible because, just like plastic, most contain harmful toxins and potential carcinogens that can seep into your child's food. Avoid aluminium, too. Although more research needs to be done, cooking with aluminium pans has been linked to Alzheimer's disease; deodorants containing aluminium have been linked to breast cancer; and aluminium has been linked to several skeletal and neurological disorders. Until this is proven right or wrong, I think it's best avoided.

Other Equipment: A good blender or small food processor is essential. You'll use it for everything from puréeing baby food to making smoothies and breadcrumbs. Get yourself a good all-round vegetable knife and an inexpensive vegetable scrubber. You shouldn't peel vegetables because much of the fibre is in the skin and a lot of nutrition is just under it, so you need to scrub them. A well-seasoned cast iron pan is great, too.

WONDERFOODS

When you're busy it's easy to cook the same thing again and again. We all do it. The recipes in this book will help to keep you on track. The wonderfoods in the chart below are nutritional powerhouses, so try to include a variety of them in your child's diet as often as you can.

FOOD	MAIN NUTRIENTS	BENEFITS TO CHILDREN	INTRODUCE THIS FOOD AT
apples	vitamin C, pectin, malic and tartaric acid	detoxifiers	6–9 months
almonds	vitamin E, potassium and magnesium; high in monounsaturated fat	aid absorption of calcium	1–2 years
avocado	oleic acid, potassium, folate, lutein, vitamin E	anti-cancer	6–9 months
broccoli	indoles, carotenoids, iron	anti-cancer	6–9 months
oily fish	omega-3 fats, EPA and protein	build brain and nerve tissue	6–9 months
pumpkin and squash	antioxidants, including beta-carotene and the rest of the carotenoids	protect against infection	6–9 months
seeds	omega-6 and omega-3 fats, zinc, magnesium and calcium	anti-cancer; reduce risk of allergies and eczema	oil, from 6–9 months; ground or chopped, from 1–2 years
seaweeds	vitamin K, iodine, chlorophyll and alginic acid	aid good thyroid function; detoxifiers	6–9 months, for cooking beans; 1–2 years, for direct feeding
sprouted beans and sprouted seeds	enzymes	improve digestion	9–12 months
whole grains	fibre, B vitamins, iron, magnesium and selenium	aid regular bowel function	6–9 months
live, natural yogurt	healthy bacteria; protein; calcium; phosphorus; vitamins B2, B12, B5; zinc	strengthens immune system	6–9 months

MAXIMIZING NUTRIENTS DURING COOKING

The recipes in this book focus heavily on nutrient-rich whole foods. Here are a few basic techniques that will help you master the art of cooking them.

SOAKING

Whole Grains: Soaking grains maximizes their nutrients and aids digestion. All grains contain phytic acid in their outer layer, which can combine with minerals in the intestinal tract and block their absorption, leading, in time, to mineral deficiencies. Soaking grains for at least seven hours or, even better, overnight, stimulates the grain's enzymes, which break down and neutralize the phytic acid. Once neutralized, phytic acid can be an important anti-cancer nutrient. Soaking also partially breaks down the proteins in grains, particularly gluten, to make them easier to digest. To soak whole grains, put the amount of grain you plan to cook in a saucepan and cover with the amount of warm water stated in the recipe. Stir in one tablespoon of kefir or yogurt and leave to soak for seven hours or overnight, then cook without draining. If there is any history of dairy allergies in your family, rinse the grains before cooking.

Dried Beans: Soak dried beans overnight in double the amount of warm water and two tablespoons of lemon juice or vinegar. This rehydrates the beans and neutralizes the phytic acid and enzyme inhibitors. The next day, rinse the beans well, add fresh water for cooking, bring to the boil and boil for ten minutes, skimming any scum, which contains the difficult-to-digest complex sugars. Then add kombu, a seaweed that helps soften the beans, makes them easier to digest and adds nutrients and flavour.

STEAMING

If you're not going to eat vegetables raw, steaming is the best way to cook them. When you boil vegetables, it is very easy to overcook them and lose valuable minerals. Steaming allows nutrients that are lost in other types of cooking to be retained. Until your baby is able to chew his food, vegetables should be steamed until completely soft; once he's chewing well, they should always be slightly crunchy.

TIME TO FEED YOUR BABY

Your baby's immune and digestive systems are still developing and are very delicate in the first two years, so start weaning slowly. Start with one food at a time. This makes it easier to identify the source of any reaction your baby might have, which is harder to do if he eats four or five different foods in one day and then develops a splotchy face, for example. If you're serving one food at time and your baby has a reaction, you can simply stop serving that food and try again after eight weeks to see if he can handle it then.

WHEN TO INTRODUCE FOODS

Raw fruit is an excellent way to start weaning because it's gentle on the baby's system, easy to digest and very nutritious. In addition to fruit, offer vegetables, whole grains, pulses and good fats from six months. To give your baby's system time to get used to solid foods, wait until a couple of months later to introduce fish and meats. Don't introduce grains such as wheat, rye and spelt until one year because they contain gluten. Gluten is one of the most common proteins to which people are intolerant, so it makes sense to wait until your baby's system is more developed. As you'll see, there is a huge range of gluten-free foods you can choose from. Eggs, cheese, nuts and certain fruits and vegetables are introduced between 12 and 24 months. See the charts in chapters 1–3 to determine if a food is appropriate at a specific age.

If you're introducing foods in the sequence I recommend and you do sometimes have to use jarred food, be aware that many contain ingredients such as milk or gluten that you won't want to introduce to your baby until a certain age. Always read the labels and buy organic.

EATING ENOUGH

Babies have a strong survival instinct and will usually eat unless they're full or something is wrong, so feed your baby until he won't eat any more. At the beginning, he may eat only one or two spoonfuls at each meal, or he may eat a whole mashed banana. It doesn't matter. It depends on your baby. Give him as much as he'll eat. If he turns his head away or won't open his mouth after one mouthful or after ten, then stop. Distract him with a toy, then try again.

Some babies eat and then need a little break before taking more. If he still won't eat, just stop and try again at the next meal. Food is new to him and his stomach is tiny. He'll gradually eat more – and you'll figure it out together.

Let your baby have a small toy at meals when he's little and he'll be happier to sit still and eat. Take the toys away when he begins feeding himself – his hands will be busy. For babies and toddlers who may not eat much at meal times, offer snacks during the day to make sure they're getting enough food and variety. You can cut out the snacking when they're older. Not all babies are chubby; many are long and slender, so don't compare yours to others. If you're worried that your baby isn't eating enough, take his weight each month and plot his progress on a growth chart. As long as he stays in the same percentile, he's fine. If he's not maintaining the same percentile, consult your doctor.

DIGESTION

Introducing foods in the sequence suggested in each chapter is the best way to ensure that your baby digests foods easily and thoroughly. Sometimes babies cry or get windy or doubled over from an upset tummy. Remember that they have the same length of intestines that we have, crammed into a really tiny space. Eating and digesting is not always easy for them. If your baby is uncomfortable, gently rub your hand in a clockwise circle from his belly button downwards and back up to help move things through his system. You can also try giving him cooled fennel tea, in a bottle or by the spoonful, to help ease digestion.

STORING & REHEATING FOOD

You'll find that many of the purées in this book are incredibly easy to make. You don't have to worry about weighing or measuring out most ingredients because when you're steaming, puréeing and freezing a butternut squash, for example, it doesn't really matter how big the squash is. The more you cook at one time, though, the easier meals will be – as long as you have storage space in your freezer. I guarantee you will use everything you make. This means that many of the purée recipes in this book don't make a specific number of servings.

How many meals a batch of Baby Brown Rice lasts really depends on how much your baby eats and how you eventually combine it with other ingredients.

Each recipe includes storage instructions, so you can plan ahead. I suggest making batches of food in the first few months and freezing them in ice-cube trays. When they're frozen, pop them out into containers that you can label and date. This will save you lots of time and provide you with a variety of foods that you can mix and match when you don't have the time or energy to cook fresh. Little cubes of fruit, vegetables and grains defrost quickly, either in the fridge or heated in a pan over a medium heat, and some can be heated simply by putting your baby's bowl in a larger bowl of boiling water, which also keeps the food warm while you feed. Rice, however, should always be heated through until it's hot, to kill any bacteria. Always thoroughly defrost meat, poultry and fish cubes in the fridge before reheating.

FOOD SAFETY

Try not to get too obsessive about germs and bacteria. Once babies are six months old, a reasonable exposure to everyday germs is a good thing because it helps to build a strong immune system. Living in a sterile environment does not. Just keep things clean, don't mix raw and cooked meats, and cook eggs and meats thoroughly for little children.

AVOIDING SWEETS

Don't be tempted to give an older child junk food or sweets 'just so he eats something'. It's actually better that he doesn't eat because then he'll eat whatever you give him later, when he's hungry. It's just not worth creating bad habits. If he hasn't eaten lunch and then asks for a chocolate bar in the afternoon, don't give in. If you do, he'll ask for it all the time. Sometimes you can avoid the argument or distract him by ignoring the request and cutting up an apple or other fruit he likes and putting it on the table without saying anything. I like to have a bowl of fruit, nuts, seeds and healthy snacks such as wholemeal pretzels, crispbreads or brown rice crackers on the table or the worktop where the children can see it, so they can help themselves. I don't offer a lot of desserts. There's no reason to have something sweet twice a day; it sets up a habit that can be difficult to reverse. When there is no dessert at the end of a meal, your child is less likely to refuse to eat his food just because he knows dessert is coming.

ADDING NUTRITION

Add nutrition wherever you can. Here are some tricks to adding a little more oomph to each day (these all must be age appropriate).

- Always serve healthy fats (see page 9). Mix good oil into purées, pasta or steamed veggies. Sprinkle seeds or toasted nori over rice or salads. Add chopped bean sprouts to sandwiches. Use yogurt with breakfast cereals or mix it with cucumber for a snack.
- Focus on healthy snacks, such as crispbreads, unsweetened popcorn and low-salt tortilla chips. Organic nuts, seeds and spreads, such as tahini, are great, too. Avoid peanuts, though – they're a pesticide-laden crop. If you do serve them, buy organic.
- At meals, offer two vegetables of different colours, one cooked and one raw, to provide different nutrients. You can serve one before the main dish. Vegetable sticks with olive oil, mayonnaise, mustard or hummus for dipping are great. Use ketchup occasionally for variety, but it's sweet, so don't become too dependent on it.
- Even if your child has a great diet, it's worth considering a good-quality, food-state multi-mineral and vitamin to ensure that he's getting everything he needs.

AND FINALLY

One of the biggest lessons to learn is to not get stressed. I can't say this enough to any mother. Do the best you can. Have some great days, don't worry about the not-so-great ones and strive to improve. Establish a routine with your child when you can. His system gets used to eating, napping and sleeping at certain times, and the steadier the routine, the easier life is. Give your child the best food you can. Try to make as many mouthfuls as you can count towards his health and well-being. He may rebel when he's older and eat rubbish for a while, but kids tend to go back to what they know – and what makes them feel good. Use this book to give your baby the best possible start in life, and to create health, vitality and happiness for a lifetime.

Chapter 1

6–9 MONTHS

By six months, your baby needs to extend her culinary range beyond breast milk or formula. If your baby is desperate for food earlier than this, you may need to start introducing fruits without seeds and non-fibrous vegetables, puréed and/or cooked as described in this chapter. Her digestive system is still developing, so start gently. Puréed fruits, vegetables, whole grains and pulses are ideal for the initial stages of weaning. From sweet Apple Purée to nutty Baby Brown Rice Purée, these first foods will give your baby the best nutritional start. When your baby gets used to eating from a spoon, make things more interesting by combining flavours and introducing a bigger variety of pulses along with fish, poultry and meat. This is the beginning of your child's relationship with food. Give her the best you can, with lots of variety, and she'll be on her way to a lifetime of good eating.

Amaranth Purée (see page 25)

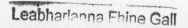

Starting your baby on her first foods is an exciting time. Begin weaning using the foods listed in the chart opposite. Take it slowly to give your child a gentle transition to solid foods.

TEXTURE

At this stage, raw fruit should be puréed or mashed until very smooth, and dried fruit should be cooked until completely soft before puréeing. All other foods should be steamed (see page 13) until completely soft, then puréed. The puréed texture should be smooth and runny like yogurt, with no lumps, and the food should always be served warm. Instant millet or brown rice flakes can be useful for thickening a meal if it's too runny. When your child starts to show an interest in chewing, gradually start to leave her purées a little lumpier by puréeing for a shorter time or by mashing them with a fork. If she starts pooping out lumps, go back to smoother purées until she is chewing more. Once she is chewing lumps, you can start mixing finely grated raw fruits and vegetables into her food. Because you're grating fruit so finely, you can also start to include the skins, which have great nutritional value. Along with the lumpier purées, you can offer your baby little pieces, about 5mm/¼in, of well-cooked vegetables or peeled soft fruit.

BREAST MILK, FORMULA AND WATER

Carry on giving your baby breast milk or formula at breakfast and between meals because it's still an important source of protein. You can also start to offer a little filtered water at mealtimes – make sure to serve it slightly warm so it doesn't chill your baby's stomach.

SOURCES OF PROTEIN

Fish is an excellent source of protein and essential fatty acids. The best to introduce are fresh anchovies (tinned are too salty) and sardines. Their tiny, soft bones provide calcium but pose no choking risk. Avoid conventionally farmed fish such as cod, which is raised in poor conditions and may carry toxins. Instead try sustainably fished alternatives such as pollock and haddock. You can also introduce organic poultry and meat, which do not contain hormones or antibiotics, and game, which is wild and lean. Make sure all meats are completely cooked.

FATS

Add two teaspoons of cold-pressed oil to your baby's food each day. Their brain and nervous systems are still developing, and the essential fats in these oils are extremely important.

OATS

You can also bring in gluten-free oats. Traditionally, oats were handled with machines that handle gluten-containing grains and were thought to contain it, but where kept isolated, oats do not contain gluten. They do contain a gluten-like protein that very sensitive people may react to.

FOODS TO BEGIN WITH AT 6–9 MONTHS

FRUITS*
*remove all skins
apple (cooked or raw)
apricot (fresh or dried)
avocado (after 4 weeks)
banana
lemon juice,
  only for soaking pulses
mango
nectarine
papaya
peach
pear
plum
....

VEGETABLES
artichoke heart
beetroot
broccoli
butternut squash
carrot
cauliflower
courgette
green bean
kombu,
  only for cooking pulses
mangetout
parsnip
pea
pumpkin
swede
sweet potato
turnip
....

GRAINS
amaranth
brown rice
buckwheat
gluten-free oats
millet
quinoa
....

PULSES
black bean
black-eyed bean
broad bean (no skins)
cannellini bean
chickpea
flageolet bean
haricot bean
lentil, including
  brown, green, red, Puy
mung bean
pinto bean
....

DAIRY & EGGS
*only for soaking
  grains
kefir
yogurt
....

FATS
serve 2 teaspoons per day
of cold-pressed seed oil
mixed with food;
choose from:
flax, hemp, olive,
  pumpkin, safflower,
  sesame, sunflower
....

NUTS
coconut
....

FISH (after 2 months)
anchovy,
  (fresh not tinned)
mackerel
salmon
sardine
....

POULTRY & MEAT*
(after 2 months)
*serve all meats
  and poultry in small
  amounts only
beef and other red meats
poultry
venison and other game

001 **Apple Purée**

Raw fruit is the easiest food for your baby to digest – and it's packed with living nutrition. You can also use this recipe for apricot, mango, nectarine, papaya, peach, pear or plum purée. Each fruit is great on its own as a snack or mixed with a grain purée for a healthy breakfast.

PREP TIME: 5 mins

1 apple, peeled, cored and chopped

1 Put the apple in a blender and blend for 1 minute until smooth, adding a little water if the mixture is too dry.

2 Serve immediately to prevent the apple discolouring.

STORAGE: Refrigerate the purée for up to 3 days or freeze in cubes for up to 3 months.

002 Dried Apricot Purée

Apricots sweeten food in a nutritious way and are a good source of beta-carotene. You can use prunes for this recipe, too. It's good to have some of these dense purées to hand as ice cubes that you can quickly defrost and serve warm when hunger suddenly strikes.

PREP TIME: 5 mins, plus overnight soaking   **COOK TIME:** 15 mins

175g/6oz/1 cup unsulphured dried apricots

1 Put the apricots and 350ml/12fl oz/scant 1½ cups water in a small saucepan and leave to soak, covered, overnight.

2 Bring to the boil over a high heat, then reduce the heat to low and simmer, covered, for 15 minutes, stirring occasionally, until completely soft. If using a blender with a plastic container, leave the mixture to cool completely before blending.

3 Transfer the mixture to a blender and blend for 1 minute until smooth. Serve warm, reheating if necessary.

STORAGE: Refrigerate the cooled purée for up to 3 days or freeze in cubes for up to 3 months.

003 Quinoa Purée

Quinoa, the highest-protein grain, is an excellent addition to your repertoire and adds variety to your baby's diet. Quinoa must be soaked, as in this recipe, or toasted as in the recipe on page 55, before cooking.

PREP TIME: 5 mins, plus overnight soaking   **COOK TIME:** 40 mins

85g/3oz/½ cup quinoa
1 tsp natural yogurt or kefir

1 Put the quinoa, yogurt and 400ml/14fl oz/1⅔ cups warm water in a medium saucepan and leave to soak, covered, for at least 7 hours or overnight.

2 Bring to the boil over a high heat, then reduce the heat to low and simmer, covered, for 40 minutes until the quinoa is very tender. If using a blender with a plastic container, leave the quinoa to cool completely before blending.

3 Transfer the quinoa to a blender and blend for 1 minute until smooth. Serve warm, reheating if necessary.

STORAGE: Refrigerate the cooled purée for up to 3 days or freeze in cubes for up to 3 months.

004 **Amaranth Purée**

Variety is so important in a baby's diet. Adding amaranth to your rotation of grains gives you choice and a new mix of minerals and vitamins.

PREP TIME: 5 mins, plus overnight soaking   **COOK TIME:** 40 mins

100g/3½oz/½ cup amaranth
1 tsp natural yogurt or kefir

1 Put the amaranth, yogurt and 455ml/16fl oz/scant 2 cups warm water in a medium saucepan and leave to soak, covered, for at least 7 hours or overnight.
2 Bring to the boil over a high heat, then reduce the heat to low and simmer, covered, for 40 minutes, stirring occasionally so the amaranth doesn't clump to the bottom of the pan. If using a blender with a plastic container, leave the amaranth to cool completely before blending.
3 Transfer the amaranth to a blender and blend for 1 minute until smooth. Serve warm, reheating if necessary.

STORAGE: Refrigerate the cooled purée for up to 3 days or freeze in cubes for up to 3 months.

005 Millet Purée

Millet is a slightly bitter grain. Try it first with non-sweet vegetables and if your baby doesn't like it, try it again with either sweet vegetables or fruits.

PREP TIME: 5 mins, plus overnight soaking   **COOK TIME:** 45 mins

100g/3½oz/½ cup millet
1 tsp natural yogurt or kefir

1 Put the millet, yogurt and 700ml/24fl oz/2¾ cups warm water in a medium saucepan and leave to soak, covered, for at least 7 hours or overnight.
2 Bring to the boil over a high heat, then reduce the heat to low and simmer, covered, for 45 minutes until completely soft. If using a blender with a plastic container, leave the millet to cool completely before blending.
3 Transfer the millet to a blender and blend for 1 minute until smooth. Serve warm, reheating if necessary.

STORAGE: Refrigerate the cooled purée for up to 3 days or freeze in cubes for up to 3 months.

006 Rice & Mango Breakfast

Brown rice flakes are a wonderful alternative to porridge oats. They cook more quickly than brown rice, making this delicious dish perfect for mornings when you're pushed for time.

PREP TIME: 10 mins, plus overnight soaking   **COOK TIME:** 10 mins

55g/2oz/½ cup brown rice flakes
1 tsp natural yogurt or kefir

1 mango, peeled, pitted and chopped
¼ apple, peeled and grated, to serve

1 Put the rice flakes, yogurt and 185ml/6fl oz/¾ cup warm water in a medium saucepan and leave to soak, covered, for at least 7 hours or overnight.

2 Bring to a simmer over a medium heat, then reduce the heat to low and cook for 10 minutes, stirring occasionally, until the rice flakes are very soft.

3 Meanwhile, put the mango in a blender and blend for 1 minute until smooth. Stir the puréed mango into the porridge, then sprinkle with the grated apple. Serve warm.

STORAGE: Refrigerate the mango purée for up to 3 days or freeze in cubes for up to 3 months. Refrigerate the cooled porridge for up to 1 day. Reheat until hot.

007 Baby Brown Rice Purée

Many parents buy white rice flakes, but your baby gets much better nutrition when you make your own brown rice purée.

PREP TIME: 5 mins, plus overnight soaking   **COOK TIME:** 1 hour

100g/3½oz/½ cup brown basmati rice
1 tsp natural yogurt or kefir

1 Put the rice, yogurt and 570ml/20fl oz/scant 2⅓ cups warm water in a medium saucepan and leave to soak, covered, for at least 7 hours or overnight.

2 Bring to the boil over a high heat, then reduce the heat to low and simmer, covered, for 1 hour until the rice is very tender. If using a blender with a plastic container, leave the rice to cool completely before blending.

3 Transfer the rice to a blender and blend for 1 minute until smooth. Serve warm, reheating if necessary.

STORAGE: Refrigerate the cooled purée for up to 1 day or freeze in cubes for up to 1 month. Reheat until hot.

008 **Artichoke Heart Purée**

This lovely purée is a nice way to introduce your baby to artichokes. Add them in small quantities to other dishes until your baby is a toddler, and old enough to enjoy them roasted or baked.

PREP TIME: 10 mins   **COOK TIME:** 45 mins

2 globe artichokes, stems removed

1 Put the artichokes in a steamer and steam, covered, over boiling water for 45 minutes until a leaf pulled from the top comes out easily. Add extra boiling water during steaming if necessary. Remove from the heat and set aside until cool enough to handle, reserving the steam water.
2 Peel the leaves off the artichokes and reserve them to serve as a starter for yourself, dipped in olive oil or melted butter. Using a sharp knife, carefully cut out and discard the hairy chokes, then chop the artichoke hearts and transfer them to a blender (leaving them to cool completely first if using a blender with a plastic container). Add enough of the reserved steam water to cover the artichoke hearts halfway. Blend for 1 minute until smooth. Serve warm, reheating if necessary.

STORAGE: Refrigerate the cooled purée for up to 3 days or freeze in cubes for up to 3 months.

009 **Carrot Purée**

You can use vegetables such as peas, courgettes and unpeeled parsnips and sweet potatoes in this recipe, but you'll need to watch the cooking times and reduce the time for courgettes (15 minutes) and peas (7 minutes).

PREP TIME: 10 mins   **COOK TIME:** 25 mins

6 carrots, unpeeled and chopped

1 Put the carrots in a steamer and steam, covered, over boiling water for 20–25 minutes until completely soft. Reserve the steam water. If using a blender with a plastic container, leave the carrots to cool completely before blending.

2 Transfer the carrots to a blender and add enough of the reserved steam water to cover them halfway. Blend for 1 minute until smooth. Serve warm, reheating if necessary.

STORAGE: Refrigerate the cooled purée for up to 3 days or freeze in cubes for up to 3 months.

010 **Red Lentil Purée**

Lentils are easy to digest and add protein to a meal. They're a great staple to have in your freezer to bulk up baby meals. Use up to three frozen cubes mixed with rice and vegetables.

PREP TIME: 5 mins, plus overnight soaking   **COOK TIME:** 55 mins

100g/3½oz/½ cup split red lentils
2 tsp lemon juice

1 Put the lentils and lemon juice in a medium saucepan, cover with water and leave to soak, covered, overnight.
2 Drain and rinse the lentils. Return them to the pan and add 455ml/16fl oz/scant 2 cups water. Bring to the boil over a high heat and boil for 10 minutes, skimming any scum that rises to the surface. Reduce the heat to low and simmer, covered, for 45 minutes until completely soft. If using a blender with a plastic container, leave the mixture to cool completely before blending.
3 Transfer the lentils and cooking liquid to a blender and blend for 1 minute until smooth. Serve warm, reheating if necessary.

STORAGE: Refrigerate the cooled purée for up to 3 days or freeze in cubes for up to 3 months.

011 **Butternut Squash Purée**

Pumpkin and squash are my favourite first vegetables. They have a lovely sweetness and are easily digested by delicate little stomachs. Use this recipe for beetroot, green beans, mangetout and peeled swede and turnip, too.

PREP TIME: 10 mins   **COOK TIME:** 30 mins

1 butternut squash, peeled, deseeded
  and cut into large cubes

1 Put the squash in a steamer and steam, covered, over boiling water for 30 minutes until completely soft. Reserve the steam water. If using a blender with a plastic container, leave the squash to cool completely before blending.

2 Transfer the squash to a blender and add enough of the reserved steam water to cover it halfway. Blend for 1 minute until smooth. Serve warm, reheating if necessary.

STORAGE: Refrigerate the cooled purée for up to 3 days or freeze in cubes for up to 3 months.

HEALTH BENEFITS

BUTTERNUT SQUASH is sweet, filling and incredibly versatile. Its lovely hue comes from its beta-carotene content, which rivals even that of mangoes and cantaloupes. High in antioxidants, it may have an anti-inflammatory effect, and also contains healthy doses of fibre, magnesium, potassium and B vitamins, which contribute to bone and heart health and support the nervous and immune systems.

012 Flageolet Purée

Cooking pulses with kombu, a vitamin- and mineral-packed seaweed, helps make them more easily digestible, especially for tiny tummies.

PREP TIME: 5 mins, plus overnight soaking **COOK TIME:** 2¼ hours

85g/3oz/½ cup dried flageolet beans 1 strip of kombu, about 8 x 5cm/3 x 2in
2 tsp lemon juice

1 Put the beans and lemon juice in a medium saucepan, cover with water and leave to soak, covered, overnight.

2 Drain and rinse the beans. Return them to the pan and add 570ml/20fl oz/scant 2⅓ cups water. Bring to the boil over a high heat and boil for 10 minutes, skimming any scum that rises to the surface. Reduce the heat to low, add the kombu and simmer, covered, for 2 hours until completely soft, then discard the kombu. If using a blender with a plastic container, leave the mixture to cool completely before blending.

3 Transfer the beans and cooking liquid to a blender and blend for 1 minute until smooth, adding a little more water if necessary. Serve warm, reheating if necessary.

STORAGE: Refrigerate the cooled purée for up to 3 days or freeze in cubes for up to 3 months.

013 Broccoli & Cauliflower Purée

You can cook these separately but mixing them together makes a great combination. Save the broccoli stalk for yourself: simply cut off the hard skin and enjoy the sweet centre raw or lightly steamed.

PREP TIME: 10 mins   **COOK TIME:** 10 mins

100g/3½oz broccoli,
  cut into bite-sized florets

100g/3½oz cauliflower,
  cut into bite-sized florets

1 Put the broccoli and cauliflower in a steamer and steam, covered, over boiling water for 10 minutes until completely soft. Reserve the steam water. If using a blender with a plastic container, leave the vegetables to cool completely before blending.

2 Transfer the vegetables to a blender and add enough of the reserved steam water to cover them halfway. Blend for 1 minute until smooth. Serve warm, reheating if necessary.

STORAGE: Refrigerate the cooled purée for up to 3 days or freeze in cubes for up to 3 months.

014 **Buckwheat & Carrot**

Buckwheat's strong flavour is balanced here by sweet carrot. Some babies will love this on its own as a main course; others will prefer it as a side dish.

MAKES: 4 servings   **PREP TIME:** 5 mins, plus overnight soaking   **COOK TIME:** 25 mins

2 tbsp buckwheat
1 tsp natural yogurt or kefir

1 carrot, quartered lengthways and sliced

1 Put the buckwheat, yogurt and 185ml/6fl oz/¾ cup warm water in a small saucepan and leave to soak, covered, for at least 7 hours or overnight.
2 Add the carrot, cover, and bring to the boil over a high heat. Reduce the heat to low and simmer, covered, for 25 minutes. Leave to cool slightly, then serve warm. If desired, transfer the mixture to a blender (leaving it to cool completely first if using a blender with a plastic container), then blend for 1 minute until smooth before serving warm, reheating if necessary.

STORAGE: Refrigerate the cooled purée for up to 3 days or freeze in cubes for up to 3 months.

015 Broad Bean & Pumpkin Purée

Sweet pumpkin goes well with anything; combined with fresh broad beans, it's simply amazing. Broad beans are a particularly special treat when they're in season because they're so fresh.

MAKES: 4 servings   **PREP TIME:** 10 mins, plus making the pumpkin purée   **COOK TIME:** 10 mins

16 broad bean pods

2 portions pumpkin purée
(see Butternut Squash Purée, page 32)

1 Slit each bean pod along its seam and pop the beans out. Bring a small saucepan of water to the boil over a high heat, add the beans and boil for 10 minutes until soft. Remove from the heat, drain and leave to cool, then peel the beans and discard the tough skins.

2 Transfer the beans to a blender and add enough water to cover them halfway. Blend for 1 minute until smooth.

3 Put the pumpkin purée and 1–2 tablespoons water in a saucepan and heat over a medium heat until warm, then stir in the broad bean purée. Serve warm.

STORAGE: Refrigerate the cooled purée for up to 3 days or freeze in cubes for up to 3 months.

016 **Pinto Beans, Millet & Avocado Purée**

I love avocado with anything. Serving it with creamy pinto beans makes it a more substantial meal for your growing baby.

MAKES: 4 servings   **PREP TIME:** 5 mins, plus overnight soaking and making the purée
COOK TIME: 2¼ hours

40g/1½oz/¼ cup dried pinto beans
2 tsp lemon juice
1 strip of kombu, about 8 x 5cm/3 x 2in

½ avocado, pitted
4 portions Millet Purée (see page 26)

1 Put the beans and lemon juice in a medium saucepan, cover with warm water and leave to soak, covered, overnight.
2 Drain and rinse the beans. Return them to the pan and add 290ml/10fl oz/scant 1¼ cups water. Bring to the boil over a high heat and boil for 10 minutes, skimming any scum that rises to the surface. Reduce the heat to low, add the kombu and simmer, covered, for 2 hours until the beans are completely soft, then discard the kombu. If using a blender with a plastic container, leave the mixture to cool completely before blending.
3 Transfer the beans and cooking liquid to a blender and blend for 1 minute until smooth.
4 Scoop the avocado flesh into a blender and add enough warm water to cover it halfway. Blend for 1 minute until smooth, adding more water if necessary. Serve warm with the pinto bean and millet purées, or mix all three purées together, reheating the beans and millet if necessary.

STORAGE: Refrigerate the cooled bean purée for up to 3 days or freeze in cubes for up to 3 months.

HEALTH BENEFITS

PINTO BEANS contain cholesterol-lowering fibre, which prevents blood sugar spikes. They are an excellent and cheap source of protein.

AVOCADOS are so packed with nutrition that they can be thought of as a complete food. They are full of fibre, potassium and B vitamins.

017 **Sardines & Sweet Potato**

Sardines really are the best type of fish, so get your baby loving them from a young age. Mixing them with sweet potato will make it easy.

MAKES: 4 servings   **PREP TIME:** 10 mins   **COOK TIME:** 20 mins

1 sweet potato, unpeeled and diced
4 tinned sardines in oil or water, drained

1 Put the sweet potato in a steamer and steam, covered, over boiling water for 20 minutes until completely soft. Remove from the heat, transfer to a bowl and mash, using a fork.
2 In another bowl, mash the sardines and their bones well with a fork, then stir them into the sweet potato. Serve warm.

STORAGE: Refrigerate the cooled purée for up to 2 days or freeze in cubes for up to 1 month.

018 Salmon & Peas

If you can get them, wild salmon and organic salmon are much better than conventionally farmed fish. The peas give this dish an intense sweetness.

MAKES: 4 servings   **PREP TIME:** 5 mins   **COOK TIME:** 15 mins

2 tsp extra virgin olive oil
115g/4oz salmon fillet, rinsed

4 tbsp peas

1 Heat the olive oil in a small frying pan over a medium heat. Add the salmon, skin-side up, and cook, covered, for 5 minutes, then turn the fish over. Cook, covered, for a further 5–10 minutes until cooked through. Meanwhile, put the peas in a steamer and steam, covered, over boiling water for 10 minutes until soft. Reserve the steam water.
2 When the fish has finished cooking, remove it from the heat and set aside until cool enough to handle. Remove and discard the skin and roughly chop the salmon, checking with your fingers for bones. If using a blender with a plastic container, leave both the peas and salmon to cool completely before blending.
3 Transfer the peas and salmon to a blender and add enough of the reserved steam water to cover them halfway. Blend for 1 minute until the mixture forms a lumpy purée. Serve warm, reheating if necessary.

STORAGE: Refrigerate the cooled purée for up to 2 days or freeze in cubes for up to 1 month.

019 Chicken & Courgette

This delicious dish is sure to be a hit. Use organic chicken, especially for a baby. It is superior in quality, texture and taste and won't contain antibiotic residues.

MAKES: 4 servings   **PREP TIME:** 5 mins   **COOK TIME:** 10 mins

2 tsp extra virgin olive oil

1 boneless, skinless chicken breast, about 100g/3½oz, coarsely chopped

½ courgette, quartered lengthways and sliced

1 Heat the olive oil in a small frying pan over a medium heat. Add the chicken and courgette and cook, covered, for 10 minutes, stirring occasionally, until the courgette is soft and the chicken is cooked through and the juices run clear. If using a blender with a plastic container, leave the mixture to cool completely before blending.

2 Transfer the chicken and courgette to a blender and blend for 1–2 minutes until slightly chunky, or longer for a smoother consistency, adding a little water if necessary. Serve warm, reheating if necessary.

STORAGE: Refrigerate the cooled purée for up to 2 days or freeze in cubes for up to 1 month.

020 **Beef & Cauliflower**

Organic beef is more expensive than conventional because it's a much higher-quality product. It's better to eat beef less frequently and eat it organically than to eat cheap conventional meat more often.

MAKES: 4 servings   **PREP TIME:** 5 mins   **COOK TIME:** 15 mins

40g/1½oz cauliflower,
  cut into bite-sized florets

1 tsp extra virgin olive oil
100g/3½oz lean beef mince

1 Put the cauliflower in a steamer and steam, covered, over boiling water for 15 minutes until completely soft. Reserve the steam water. Meanwhile, heat the olive oil in a small frying pan over a medium heat. Add the mince and cook for 10 minutes, stirring occasionally, until thoroughly cooked through. If using a blender with a plastic container, leave both the beef and cauliflower to cool completely before blending.

2 Transfer the beef and cauliflower to a blender. Blend for 1 minute, slowly adding a little of the reserved steam water 1 tablespoon at a time, until smooth. Serve warm, reheating if necessary.

STORAGE: Refrigerate the cooled purée for up to 2 days or freeze in cubes for up to 1 month.

Chapter 2

9–12 MONTHS

By 9 to 12 months your baby's appetite is really growing! He's now getting the majority of his calories from food rather than breast milk or formula, so it's more important than ever to optimize nutrition. Seeded fruits, such as raspberries, are a great addition to his diet. Live natural yogurt is no longer just for soaking – your baby can eat it now on its own or mixed into food. At this age, he'll be ready to put his new teeth to use on more textured foods, so you can gradually start phasing out purées and offer little bits of food instead. Remember that variety is key in helping your baby to develop a love of good food. A colourful Saucy Steam-Fry and flavourful Grilled Onion Chicken are just some of the delicious options he's now ready to devour.

Pollock with Green Beans (see page 66)

The amount of food your baby is eating now can be quite impressive. A good ratio to follow at this age is one part starch to one part vegetable, plus good seed oil and some protein. Add extra nutrition to your child's meals wherever you can. For example, sprinkle beans and grains with finely chopped herbs, such as parsley or basil. Your child is now ready for the foods listed in the chart below. Combine these with the foods listed in the previous chapters to give your baby the best variety you can.

TEXTURE

At this age, most children will be able to handle more texture in their food. You may be able to stop puréeing meals altogether, or you may have to purée them only a little. If your baby wasn't interested in finely grated or small pieces of raw fruits and vegetables before, he should be able to eat them now, and you can leave the skins on. As your baby's motor skills develop, finger foods will become more interesting. He might now be able to manage some pieces of peach, grapes or cucumber, peeled and deseeded. Cut fruit or vegetables into 5mm/ ¼in pieces to prevent choking and always sit with your child during meals in case he needs your help. You can also add in fruit with little seeds now, such as kiwi and blackberries. Don't worry if your baby isn't chewing much yet and still needs a lot of things puréed. He'll get there soon.

BREAST MILK, FORMULA, YOGURT & KEFIR

Carry on with the breast milk or formula – it's an excellent food, and by this stage your baby will naturally take less. Always offer milk away from solid food, so it doesn't fill him up just before he eats. If you're using formula, follow the instructions on the packet to determine how much to give your baby at this age. You can now also introduce live, organic natural yogurt and kefir – both are good sources of calcium and protein, and they contain important probiotic bacteria that support good digestive health. Your baby's digestive system is still developing, though, so I recommend waiting a few more months before introducing other dairy products (see page 9).

FATS

Good fats continue to be important, so keep giving your child two teaspoons of cold-pressed seed oil each day. Carry on with other nutritious sources of essential fatty acids as well, such as avocado and oily fish.

SPROUTS

You can introduce sprouts now, too. Sprouts are one of the most complex, nutritious foods, rich in vitamins, minerals and proteins. Sprouts are considered 'live foods' because the seeds are germinating and growing. The nutrition in live foods is far superior to other foods. The living enzymes in the sprouts aid our digestion and our assimilation of nutrients; this also makes them very easy to digest. Toss them in the blender when you purée your baby's food or chop them and mix them into meals. You really can't overuse them and they are a phenomenal course of nutrition.

NEW FOODS TO INTRODUCE AT 9–12 MONTHS

FRUITS
blackberry
blueberry
cranberry (fresh or
  unsweetened dried)
currant
date
fig
grape
kiwi
lychee
raisin
raspberry
rhubarb

....
VEGETABLES
asparagus
Chinese leaf
cucumber
fennel
garlic
fresh herbs,
  such as basil,
  mint and parsley,
Jerusalem artichoke
onion
pak choi
spring onion

sprouts
(all types,
  including
  alfalfa, broccoli,
  chickpea and lentil)
....
GRAINS
corn
oats
....
FISH*
*avoid overfished
  varieties, such
  as cod

haddock
pollock
trout
....
DAIRY & EGGS
kefir
yogurt
....
FATS
butter

021 Berry & Oat Porridge

Soaked porridge is a family favourite – and incredibly versatile. The sweet, tart berries featured in this version will be a great flavour experience for your baby, but you can use any mixture of stewed or fresh fruits. (From 15 months you can add ground seeds and/or nuts, too.)

MAKES: 4 servings   **PREP TIME:** 5 mins, plus overnight soaking   **COOK TIME:** 10 mins

115g/4oz/1 heaped cup porridge oats
270ml/9½fl oz/1 cup plus 1 tbsp
    natural yogurt

125g/4½oz/1 cup berries, such as
    raspberries, blueberries or blackberries

1 Put the oats and 1 tablespoon yogurt in a small saucepan. Add 750ml/26fl oz/3 cups water and leave to soak, covered, for at least 7 hours or overnight.
2 Bring the soaked oats to a simmer over a medium heat, then reduce the heat to low and cook for 10 minutes, stirring occasionally, until soft and creamy. Remove from the heat.
3 Mix in the remaining yogurt and berries. If the mixture is too coarse, transfer it to a blender and blend for 1 minute until smooth (leaving it to cool completely first if using a blender with a plastic container). Serve warm, reheating if necessary.

STORAGE: Refrigerate the cooled porridge for up to 3 days or freeze for up to 3 months.

022 Gluten-Free Porridge with Dates

This easy and delicious porridge uses three gluten-free grains. It's one of my favourite creations and makes an ideal start to the day, especially in the colder months.

MAKES: 4 servings   **PREP TIME:** 5 minutes   **COOK TIME:** 15 minutes

3 tbsp millet flakes

3 tbsp quinoa flakes

3 tbsp buckwheat flakes

3 tbsp chopped dried dates

1 Put all of the ingredients and 455ml/16fl oz/scant 2 cups water in a medium saucepan. Bring to a simmer over a medium heat, then reduce the heat to low and cook for 15 minutes, stirring continuously, until soft. Remove from the heat and leave to cool a little. Serve warm. If a smoother consistency is desired, transfer the mixture to a blender (leaving it to cool completely first if using a blender with a plastic container) and blend for 1 minute until smooth. Serve warm, reheating if necessary.

STORAGE: Refrigerate the cooled porridge for up to 3 days or freeze for up to 3 months

023 **Fruit Ambrosia**

You could serve this versatile recipe with cooked grains instead of millet flakes if you prefer. It makes a fabulous base for smoothies, too: just omit the millet flakes and add any other fruits from this or the previous chapter to create a great mid-morning or mid-afternoon drink snack.

MAKES: 2 servings   **PREP TIME:** 10 mins

1 banana, peeled
55g/2oz seedless red grapes
1 kiwi, peeled and roughly chopped

4 tbsp Greek yogurt
4 tbsp instant millet flakes

1 Put the banana, grapes, kiwi and yogurt in a blender and pulse a few times until lumpy.
2 Divide the mixture into two bowls, then stir 2 tablespoons of the millet flakes into each portion and serve.

STORAGE: Refrigerate for up to 1 day.

HEALTH BENEFITS

MILLET is one of the oldest foods known and possibly the first cereal grain used. It is alkaline and helps balance acidity in the body. It is also easy to digest, helps bowel function and is calming.

BANANAS are one of nature's best sources of potassium, which helps to regulate salt in the body and is valuable when your baby has diarrhoea. Their pectin content can also help to relieve constipation.

YOGURT is a health-promoting wonderfood that gives your baby good bacteria, protein, calcium, vitamin B12 and other nutrients. Offer it plain or mixed with cereals and fruits.

024 Quinoa & Coconut Porridge

Porridge is not only made with oats. Remember amaranth, brown rice, buckwheat, millet and quinoa when you need creative breakfast ideas.

MAKES: 4 servings   **PREP TIME:** 5 mins, plus overnight soaking and making the apricot purée
COOK TIME: 40 mins

170g/6oz/1 cup quinoa
4 tbsp flaked coconut
2 tbsp natural yogurt or kefir

4 tsp Dried Apricot Purée (see page 23),
 to serve

1 Put the quinoa, coconut, yogurt and 700ml/24fl oz/generous 2¾ cups warm water in
  a medium saucepan and leave to soak, covered, for at least 7 hours or overnight.
2 Bring the mixture to the boil over a high heat, then reduce the heat to low and simmer, covered,
  for 40 minutes until the quinoa is very soft. If using a blender with a plastic container, leave the
  mixture to cool completely before blending.
3 Transfer the mixture to a blender and blend for 1 minute until smooth. Serve warm with the
  apricot purée, reheating if necessary.

STORAGE: Refrigerate the cooled porridge for up to 3 days or freeze for up to 3 months.

025 **Grits**

Grits are a traditional corn dish from the American South. This gorgeous, buttery dish makes a fabulous breakfast that the entire family can enjoy. You can also serve it as a side dish – in the southern United States, it's often eaten with pork. (Once your baby has reached one year, you can add ¾ teaspoon salt in step 1.)

SERVES: 2 adults and 2 children   **PREP TIME:** 5 mins   **COOK TIME:** 20 mins

225g/8oz/1½ cups coarsely ground polenta   175g/6oz butter, cut into 6 pieces
(hominy grits)

1 In a medium saucepan, bring 1.4l/48fl oz/5½ cups water to the boil. Add the polenta and whisk quickly with a wire whisk until the mixture is smooth and has no lumps. Reduce the heat to medium-low and simmer very gently for 20 minutes, stirring with the whisk every few minutes, until thick.
2 Remove from the heat and divide into four bowls. Top each child portion with 1 piece of the butter and each adult portion with 2 pieces. Serve hot.

026 **Buttered Turnip Sauté**

Your little one won't be able to get enough of these succulent, buttery turnips. A versatile, often overlooked vegetable, turnips are great raw, too. Try serving them finely grated into salads.

MAKES: 4 servings   **PREP TIME:** 10 mins   **COOK TIME:** 10 mins

30g/1oz butter
200g/7oz turnips, quartered and sliced

1 Melt the butter in a large frying pan over a low heat. Add the turnips and cook for 10 minutes until completely soft. Stir occasionally to ensure they cook evenly.
2 Mash the turnips, using a fork, and serve warm. If a smoother consistency is desired, transfer the turnips to a blender (leaving them to cool completely first if using a blender with a plastic container) and blend for 1 minute until smooth. Serve warm, reheating if necessary.

STORAGE: Refrigerate the cooled mash for up to 3 days or freeze for up to 3 months.

027 **Quinoa, Chinese Leaf & Carrot Stew**

This colourful stew makes a quick, delicious meal. Chinese leaves are great – they can also be used finely chopped in salads and on sandwiches.

MAKES: 4 servings   **PREP TIME:** 10 mins   **COOK TIME:** 35 mins

55g/2oz/⅓ cup quinoa

1 carrot, sliced

2 heads of Chinese leaves, about 115g/4oz, chopped

1 Put the quinoa in a sieve and rinse under cold running water, then drain well. Transfer to a medium saucepan and toast over a high heat for 5 minutes, stirring continuously, until any excess water has evaporated and the quinoa has browned slightly and begun to pop.

2 Slowly add 455ml/16fl oz/scant 2 cups water and bring to the boil over a high heat. Reduce the heat to low and simmer, covered, for 10 minutes. Add the carrot and simmer, covered, for a further 10 minutes, then add the Chinese leaves. Continue simmering, covered, for a further 10 minutes until the grain and vegetables are very soft. If using a blender with a plastic container, leave the mixture to cool completely before blending.

3 Transfer the mixture to a blender. Blend for 1 minute or until the desired consistency is achieved. Serve warm, reheating if necessary.

STORAGE: Refrigerate the cooled stew for up to 3 days or freeze for up to 3 months.

028 Cannellini Beans & Amaranth

Combining creamy cannellini beans with subtly sweet amaranth makes a delicious protein meal. Amaranth has a lovely flavour and can be combined with anything.

MAKES: 4 servings   **PREP TIME:** 5 mins, plus overnight soaking and making the amaranth purée
COOK TIME: 1¾ hours

85g/3oz/½ cup dried cannellini beans
2 tsp lemon juice

1 strip of kombu, about 8 x 5cm/3 x 2in
4 portions Amaranth Purée (see page 25)

1 Put the beans and lemon juice in a medium saucepan, cover with water and leave to soak, covered, overnight.

2 Drain and rinse the beans. Return them to the pan and add 570ml/20fl oz/scant 2⅓ cups water. Bring to the boil over a high heat and boil for 10 minutes, skimming any scum that rises to the surface. Reduce the heat to low, add the kombu and simmer, covered, for 1½ hours until the beans are completely soft, then discard the kombu.

3 Mash with a fork, then mix with an equal portion of the amaranth purée and serve warm. If a smoother consistency is desired, transfer the mixture to a blender (leaving it to cool completely first if using a blender with a plastic container) and pulse for 1 minute or until the desired consistency is achieved. Serve warm, reheating if necessary.

STORAGE: Refrigerate the cooled purée for up to 3 days or freeze for up to 3 months.

029 Swede & Pak Choi

In this beautiful dish, the green pak choi creates visual appeal, while its clean, fresh flavour brightens up the more sombre swede.

MAKES: 4 servings   **PREP TIME:** 10 mins   **COOK TIME:** 25 mins

450g/1lb swede, peeled and diced
70g/2½oz pak choi, cut into thin strips

1 Put the swede in a steamer and steam, covered, over boiling water for 20 minutes until completely soft, then remove from the steamer and set aside. Reserve the steam water.

2 Put the pak choi in the steamer and steam, covered, over boiling water for 3 minutes until wilted. Reserve the steam water. If using a blender with a plastic container, leave the vegetables to cool completely before blending.

3 Transfer the vegetables to a blender and pulse for 1 minute until the mixture forms a lumpy purée, slowly adding a little of the reserved steam water if necessary. If a smoother consistency is desired, blend for a little longer. Serve warm, reheating if necessary.

STORAGE: Refrigerate the cooled purée for up to 3 days or freeze for up to 3 months.

030 Saucy Steam-Fry

The visual impact of food is important for children. The bright, colourful vegetables cut into pretty shapes in this dish will catch your baby's eye and get him excited about his meal.

MAKES: 4 servings   **PREP TIME:** 15 mins   **COOK TIME:** 20 mins

2 tsp kuzu
1 tbsp toasted sesame oil
1 carrot, quartered lengthways and sliced
55g/2oz/1 cup dried corn pasta

55g/2oz cauliflower, cut into tiny florets
40g/1½oz broccoli, cut into tiny florets
1 tsp mirin

1 In a bowl, mix together the kuzu and 1 tablespoon cold water, stirring until the kuzu has dissolved, then set aside. Heat a wok or frying pan over a medium-low heat. Add the sesame oil, carrot and 4 tablespoons hot water. Steam-fry for 5 minutes, stirring frequently. As the pan begins to dry out, add another 4 tablespoons hot water. Cook for a further 5 minutes until the carrot has begun to soften. Meanwhile, bring a large pan of water to the boil and cook the pasta for 2 minutes longer than suggested in the packet instructions so it is very soft, then drain.

2 Add the cauliflower and 4 tablespoons hot water to the wok and steam-fry for 3 minutes, stirring frequently, until the cauliflower has begun to soften. Add the broccoli and another 4 tablespoons hot water and continue steam-frying for 5 minutes, stirring occasionally.

3 Stir the kuzu mixture and mirin into the vegetables and cook for a further 2 minutes, stirring, until the vegetables are tender and the sauce is thick and shimmery. Remove from the heat.

4 Divide the pasta into four bowls and top each portion with one-quarter of the steam-fry. Serve warm. If a smoother consistency is desired, transfer the pasta and vegetables to a blender (leaving them to cool completely first if using a blender with a plastic container) and pulse a few times until lumpy. Serve warm, reheating if necessary.

STORAGE: Refrigerate for up to 3 days.

HEALTH BENEFITS

KUZU is an outstanding gelling and thickening agent that also has soothing medicinal effects. It can relieve digestive problems, and its high flavonoid content aids circulation by helping to dilate blood vessels.

BROCCOLI lessens the effect of allergens in our bodies, metabolizes vitamin D and also helps the body to detox. Try to serve it up to three times a week, but steam it rather than boil it to ensure it retains its goodness.

031 **Puy Lentils & Butternut Squash**

This beautiful combination of savoury lentils and naturally sweet butternut squash is sure to become a favourite with your baby.

MAKES: 4 servings **PREP TIME:** 10 mins, plus overnight soaking **COOK TIME:** 1¼ hours

100g/3½oz/½ cup dried Puy lentils
2 tsp lemon juice

1 small butternut squash, peeled, deseeded
 and chopped
1 tbsp extra virgin olive oil

1 Put the lentils and lemon juice in a medium saucepan, cover with warm water and leave to soak, covered, overnight.

2 Drain and rinse the lentils. Return them to the pan and add 375ml/13fl oz/1½ cups water. Bring to the boil over a high heat and boil for 10 minutes, skimming any scum that rises to the surface. Reduce the heat to low and simmer, covered, for 1 hour until completely soft.

3 Meanwhile, preheat the oven to 200°C/400°F/Gas 6. Put the squash in a shallow baking dish, drizzle with the olive oil and toss to coat. Bake for 30–40 minutes until very soft and lightly browned. Remove from the oven. If using a blender with a plastic container, leave the squash and lentils to cool completely before blending.

4 Transfer the squash, lentils and cooking liquid to a blender. Blend for 1 minute until smooth. Serve warm, reheating if necessary.

STORAGE: Refrigerate the cooled purée for up to 3 days or freeze for up to 3 months.

032 Black-Eyed Beans & Brown Rice

A classic vegetarian protein, the combination of beans and rice forms a complete protein that has all the essential amino acids the body needs.

MAKES: 4 servings   **PREP TIME:** 5 mins, plus overnight soaking and making the brown rice purée
COOK TIME: 3¼ hours

85g/3oz/½ cup dried black-eyed beans
2 tsp lemon juice
1 strip of kombu, about 8 x 5cm/3 x 2in

4 portions Baby Brown Rice Purée
(see page 28)

1 Put the beans and lemon juice in a medium saucepan, cover with warm water and leave to soak, covered, overnight.

2 Drain and rinse the beans. Return them to the pan and add 570ml/20fl oz/scant 2⅓ cups water. Bring to the boil over a high heat and boil for 10 minutes, skimming any scum that rises to the surface. Reduce the heat to low, add the kombu and simmer, covered, for 3 hours until the beans are completely soft, then discard the kombu. If using a blender with a plastic container, leave the mixture to cool completely before blending.

3 Transfer the beans and cooking liquid to a blender and blend for 1 minute until smooth. Serve warm with the rice purée, reheating if necessary.

STORAGE: Refrigerate the cooled bean purée for up to 1 day or freeze for up to 3 months.

033 **Brown Rice & Sprouts**

One of my daughter Cassie's favourites, this dish is brilliant on its own or as a base into which you can mix other foods. Using sprouted alfalfa seeds is a lovely way to add vitality to your growing child's diet.

MAKES: 4 servings **PREP TIME:** 5 mins, plus overnight soaking **COOK TIME:** 1 hour

100g/3½oz/½ cup short grain brown rice
1 tbsp natural yogurt or kefir

1 garlic clove, crushed
55g/2oz alfalfa sprouts

1 Put the rice, yogurt and 570ml/20fl oz/scant 2⅓ cups warm water in a medium saucepan and leave to soak, covered, for at least 7 hours or overnight.
2 Add the garlic to the rice and bring to the boil over a high heat, then reduce the heat to low and simmer, covered, for 1 hour until the rice is very tender. If using a blender with a plastic container, leave the mixture to cool completely before blending.
3 Transfer the mixture to a blender, add the sprouts and blend for 1 minute until smooth. Serve warm, reheating if necessary.

STORAGE: Refrigerate the cooled purée for up to 1 day or freeze for up to 1 month. Reheat until hot.

034 Mangetout, Cucumber & Yogurt Salad

Fresh vegetables mixed with yogurt make a delicious first salad for your little one. For variation, add chopped cucumber and avocado. (From one year, you can add chopped tomato, too.)

MAKES: 1 serving   **PREP TIME:** 10 mins   **COOK TIME:** 10 mins

4 mangetout, cut into bite-sized pieces
40g/1½oz cucumber, peeled, deseeded
  and cut into bite-sized pieces

1 tsp natural yogurt

1 Put the mangetout in a steamer and steam, covered, over boiling water for 10 minutes until soft. Remove from the heat and leave to cool completely.
2 Put the mangetout, cucumber and yogurt in a small bowl, mix well and serve. If a smoother consistency is desired, transfer the mixture to a blender and pulse a few times until the desired consistency is achieved, then serve.

035 **Haricot Beans & Beetroot**

Beetroot's natural sweetness beautifully complements haricot beans. This is a good dish
to have on the side or to mix with a grain, such as quinoa or millet, to make a main dish.

MAKES: 4 servings   **PREP TIME:** 10 mins, plus overnight soaking   **COOK TIME:** 1¾ hours

85g/3oz/½ cup dried haricot beans
2 tsp lemon juice
1 strip of kombu, about 8 x 5cm/3 x 2in

4 small beetroots with stalks, washed well
and stalks trimmed to 2.5cm/1in

1 Put the beans and lemon juice in a medium saucepan, cover with warm water and leave
to soak, covered, overnight.

2 Drain and rinse the beans. Return them to the pan and add 570ml/20fl oz/scant 2⅓ cups
water. Bring to the boil over a high heat and boil for 10 minutes, skimming any scum that rises
to the surface. Reduce the heat to low, add the kombu and simmer, covered, for 1½ hours until
the beans are completely soft, then discard the kombu. If using a blender with a plastic
container, leave the mixture to cool completely before blending.

3 Meanwhile, bring a medium saucepan of water to the boil over a high heat and add the
beetroots, ensuring they are completely covered in water. Reduce the heat to low and simmer,
covered, for 45 minutes until the beetroots are completely soft and the skins come off easily.
Drain and leave to stand until cool enough to handle.

4 Remove and discard the skins, then chop the beetroots, put them in a blender and blend for
1 minute until smooth, adding a little water if necessary. Transfer the purée to a bowl and
wash the blender.

5 Transfer the beans and cooking liquid to the blender and blend for 1 minute until smooth.

6 Mix together equal quantities of the bean and beetroot purées. Serve warm, reheating
if necessary.

STORAGE: Refrigerate the cooled purées for up to 3 days or freeze for up to 3 months.

036 Mung Beans with Toasted Quinoa

Mung beans are easily digested, so they're perfect for your baby. Combining beans and grains is a wonderful way to get protein, so mix and match to create a range of healthy meals.

MAKES: 4 servings   **PREP TIME:** 5 mins, plus overnight soaking   **COOK TIME:** 1¼ hours

85g/3oz/½ cup dried mung beans
2 tsp lemon juice

1 strip of kombu, about 8 x 5cm/3 x 2in
85g/3oz/½ cup quinoa

1 Put the beans and lemon juice in a medium saucepan, cover with warm water and leave to soak, covered, overnight.

2 Drain and rinse the beans. Return them to the pan and add 570ml/20fl oz/scant 2⅓ cups water. Bring to the boil over a high heat and boil for 10 minutes, skimming any scum that rises to the surface. Reduce the heat to low, add the kombu and simmer, covered, for 1 hour until the beans are completely soft, then discard the kombu.

3 Meanwhile, put the quinoa in a sieve and rinse under cold running water, then drain well. Transfer to a medium saucepan and toast over a high heat for 5 minutes, stirring continuously, until any excess water has evaporated and the quinoa has browned slightly and begun to pop. Slowly add 240ml/8fl oz/scant 1 cup water, cover and bring to the boil over a high heat. Reduce the heat to low and simmer for 30 minutes until tender. If using a blender with a plastic container, leave both the quinoa and the bean mixture to cool completely before blending.

4 Transfer the bean mixture to a blender and blend for 1 minute until smooth. Transfer the purée to a bowl and wash the blender.

5 Put the quinoa in the blender and blend for 1 minute until smooth.

6 Mix together equal quantities of the bean and quinoa purées. Serve warm, reheating if necessary.

STORAGE: Refrigerate the cooled purées for up to 3 days or freeze for up to 3 months.

037 **Pollock with Green Beans**

Pollock is a mild, lean, tender fish. The fillets are usually bone-free with a consistent snow-white colour. It flakes easily, making it perfect for kids – and it's a great alternative to overfished cod.

MAKES: 4 servings   **PREP TIME:** 10 mins   **COOK TIME:** 15 mins

100g/3½oz green beans,
   trimmed and chopped

1½ tsp extra virgin olive oil
100g/3½oz pollock fillet, rinsed

1 Put the green beans in a steamer and steam, covered, over boiling water for 15 minutes until completely soft. If using a blender with a plastic container, leave to cool completely before blending.

2 Meanwhile, heat ½ teaspoon of the olive oil in a small frying pan over a medium heat. Add the pollock, skin-side up, and cook, covered, for 5 minutes, then turn the fish over and cook, covered, for a further 5–10 minutes until white and cooked through. Remove from the heat and set aside until cool enough to handle.

3 Remove and discard the skin and roughly chop the fish, checking with your fingers for bones, then transfer to a bowl and mash with a fork. If a smoother consistency is desired, transfer the fish to a blender (leaving it to cool completely first if using a blender with a plastic container) and blend for 1 minute until smooth.

4 Transfer the beans to a clean blender, add the remaining olive oil and pulse for 1 minute until the mixture forms a lumpy purée. Serve warm with the fish, reheating if necessary.

STORAGE: Refrigerate the fish for up to 2 days or freeze for up to 1 month. Refrigerate the beans for up to 3 days or freeze for up to 3 months.

038 Mackerel & Broccoli

Your baby will love the rich texture of nutrient-rich mackerel. Serve this as suggested or mix it with a grain to add some complex carbohydrates.

MAKES: 4 servings   **PREP TIME:** 5 mins   **COOK TIME:** 10 mins

115g/4oz broccoli, cut into bite-sized florets
85g/3oz smoked mackerel, deboned

1 Put the broccoli in a steamer and steam, covered, over boiling water for 10 minutes until completely soft. Reserve the steam water. If using a blender with a plastic container, leave to cool completely before blending.

2 Meanwhile, remove and discard the skin from the mackerel and remove any remaining bones, feeling the flesh with your fingers. Shred the mackerel into a small bowl with a fork.

3 Transfer the broccoli to a blender and add enough of the reserved steam water to cover it halfway. Add the mackerel and blend for 1 minute until smooth, adding more steam water if necessary. Serve warm, reheating if necessary.

STORAGE: Refrigerate the cooled purée for up to 2 days or freeze for up to 1 month.

039 Grilled Onion Chicken

Grilling brings out great flavours in the onion and the chicken. Use organic chicken and you get meat with less water and more flavour.

MAKES: 4 servings   **PREP TIME:** 5 mins   **COOK TIME:** 11 mins

2 tsp extra virgin olive oil

110g/4oz boneless, skinless chicken breast,
   cut into small chunks

1 large onion, finely chopped

1 Preheat the grill to medium and grease a medium, shallow baking tray with the oil. Put the chicken and onion in the baking tray and grill for 6–7 minutes until the onion and chicken begin to brown.

2 Remove from the grill, stir and then grill for a further 3–4 minutes until the chicken is cooked through and the juices run clear. Serve warm.

3 If a smoother consistency is desired, transfer the chicken and onion to a blender (leaving the mixture to cool completely first if using a blender with a plastic container). Pulse for 1 minute, or until the desired consistency is achieved, then serve warm, reheating if necessary.

STORAGE: Refrigerate the cooled mixture for up to 2 days or freeze for up to 1 month.

040 **Venison & Parsnip**

Wild meats offer another healthy alternative to intensively farmed meats. Venison's strong, earthy flavour is nicely balanced here by the parsnip.

MAKES: 4 servings   **PREP TIME:** 5 mins   **COOK TIME:** 15 mins

40g/1½oz parsnip, sliced
2 tsp extra virgin olive oil

100g/3½oz venison

1 Put the parsnip in a steamer and steam, covered, over boiling water for 15 minutes until completely soft. Reserve the steam water.
2 Meanwhile, heat the olive oil in a small frying pan over a medium heat. Add the venison and cook, partially covered, for 5 minutes until beginning to brown. Turn it over and cook, partially covered, for a further 5 minutes until thoroughly cooked through. If using a blender with a plastic container, leave both the venison and parsnip to cool completely before blending.
3 Transfer the venison and parsnip to a blender. Blend for 1 minute, slowly adding a little of the reserved steam water 1 tablespoon at a time, until smooth. Serve warm, reheating if necessary.

STORAGE: Refrigerate the cooled purée for up to 2 days or freeze for up to 1 month.

Chapter 3

1–2 YEARS

Your baby will reach some remarkable developmental milestones during this period. If she hasn't already taken her first steps, she will very soon. Before you know it, she'll be off and running – with you in quick pursuit. In the coming months, she'll start talking and acquiring lots of new motor skills as well. All of this growth and energy requires fuel, and the best fuel you can continue to give her is a nutrition-packed diet. Your baby is now ready to eat all family meals and try great new foods such as potatoes, tomatoes, eggs, seeds, nuts, and whole grains like barley, rye, and spelt. With healthy and delicious options like Spelt French Toast, Polenta with Shiitake Mushrooms and Best Beef Burgers, mealtimes are about to become significantly more exciting.

Baked Frittata (see page 89)

Your baby can now eat all family meals. Continue to use salt very sparingly in your cooking, and avoid sugar as much as possible. Your child is now ready for the foods listed in the chart opposite. Combine them with the foods listed in the previous chapters to give her variety.

WEANING OFF BREAST MILK
When you wean your baby off breast milk or formula, I don't recommend replacing it with cow's milk (see page 9). Rely on yogurt and foods such as nuts and seeds and vegetables such as spinach for calcium and magnesium, or offer organic goat's or sheep's milk if you like.

CHEESE & EGGS
You can introduce cheese now; organic sheep's and goat's milk cheeses are the best options. You can also offer thoroughly cooked organic eggs, which are an excellent source of protein.

CITRUS FRUIT
Oranges and grapefruit are common allergenic foods, but at this age your child should be able to handle them. Include them in your child's diet occasionally, but keep giving her lots of other fruits, too. Don't let her drink fruit juices, though, or she'll always want that sweet flavour.

GLUTEN & WHEAT
Your baby's digestive system should be mature enough to handle gluten, so you can introduce wheat and offer pasta, but be careful not to rely on it too much. Look for wholemeal spelt or Kamut pasta and alternate with gluten-free alternatives, such as buckwheat noodles and corn pasta. Cook the pasta until soft, to make it easy for your baby to chew and digest.

NIGHTSHADES
You can go ahead with aubergines, potatoes and tomatoes. These foods do have nutritional benefits, but they also contain alkaloids, which can affect nerve-muscle function and digestive function, and compromise joint function. Add them sparingly.

NUTS & SEEDS

When your baby is chewing well, you can introduce seeds and nuts (except peanuts, which should not be introduced until age five), which contain healthy fats. Chop them up or grind them in a spice mill, then mix them into foods or snacks. Nut and seed butters are great, too.

ESSENTIAL FATTY ACID (EFA) SEED MIX

You can now make a seed mix to alternate with seed oils for added texture. Put one part each of sesame seeds and sunflower or pumpkin seeds in a jar. Add two parts of flax seeds, seal and keep in the fridge. Grind 2 tablespoons of the mixture at a time and mix into your baby's food.

SOYA

You can offer soya, but keep it to a minimum as its phytoestrogens may affect hormone balance. Tofu is fine occasionally, but tempeh is easier to digest and contains B vitamins.

NEW FOODS TO INTRODUCE AT 1–2 YEARS

FRUITS
citrus
  (in small amounts):
  clementine, grapefruit,
  kumquat, lemon,
  lime, mandarin,
  orange, pomelo,
  satsuma, tangerine
passion fruit
pomegranate
strawberry
....

VEGETABLES
aubergine
Brussels sprout
cabbage
caper
chard
gherkin
green pepper
kale
lettuce
mushroom
olive (pitted)
potato
rocket
samphire
seaweed
  (arame, hijiki,
  kombu and nori)
spinach
sweetcorn
sweet pepper
tomato
watercress
....

GRAINS
barley
Kamut
rye
spelt
wheat
....

PULSES
soya foods
  (keep to a minimum):
  tempeh
  tofu

....

NUTS & SEEDS
nuts: almond, Brazil nut,
  chestnut, hazelnut,
  macadamia nut, pecan,
  pine nut, pistachio nut,
  walnut
seeds: flax, hemp,
  pumpkin, sesame,
  sunflower
....

DAIRY & EGGS
cheese
  (especially organic):
  goat's and sheep's milk
eggs

041 **Spelt French Toast**

A great breakfast that combines complex carbs with protein – and with a little added sweetness. It's hard not to love this dish, no matter how old you are.

SERVES: 2 adults and 2 children   **PREP TIME:** 5 mins   **COOK TIME:** 20 mins

6 eggs, beaten
3 tbsp sugar
6 tbsp rice milk

¼ tsp vanilla extract
30g/1oz butter
6 slices of wholemeal spelt or wheat bread

1 Preheat the oven to 70°C/150°F/Gas ¼. Put the eggs, sugar, rice milk and vanilla extract in a shallow bowl or baking dish and mix well until the sugar has dissolved.

2 Melt the butter in a large frying pan over a medium heat. Put 1 slice of bread in the baking dish and leave to soak in the mixture for a few seconds, then turn it over and soak until moist. Put the soaked bread in the pan and repeat with another slice of bread.

3 Fry for 2–3 minutes on each side until lightly browned. Transfer to a plate and keep warm in the oven while you make the rest of the French toast. Serve warm.

042 Cornbread Pudding

My grandmother created this delicious breakfast 'pudding'. It's so moreish that it's hard to stop eating once you start, especially warm from the oven.

SERVES: 2 adults and 2 children   PREP TIME: 20 mins   COOK TIME: 45 mins

55g/2oz butter, cubed,
    plus extra for greasing
150g/5½oz/1 cup polenta
115g/4oz/½ cup sugar

375ml/13fl oz/1½ cups rice milk
2 eggs, beaten
1 tsp gluten-free baking powder
¼ tsp fine sea salt

1 Preheat the oven to 180°C/350°F/Gas 4 and grease a 20 x 20cm/8 x 8in baking dish with butter. Put the polenta in a large mixing bowl and whisk in 455ml/16fl oz/scant 2 cups boiling water, using a wire whisk.

2 Add the butter and sugar and mix with a spoon or rubber spatula until smooth and there are no lumps. Add the rice milk, eggs, baking powder and salt and mix well. Pour into the prepared baking dish.

3 Bake for 45 minutes until golden brown and firm at the edges. It will be wobbly in the middle. Remove from the oven and leave to cool for 10 minutes, then slice and serve hot, warm or cold.

STORAGE: Refrigerate for up to 3 days.

043 **Wholemeal Spelt Pancakes**

Transform the relatively unhealthy breakfast of white-flour pancakes into a nutritious – and delicious – meal by using wholemeal spelt flour. Pancakes travel well and make a great snack for a hungry toddler.

SERVES: 2 adults and 2 children   **PREP TIME**: 10 mins   **COOK TIME**: 30 mins

325g/11½oz/2¾ cups wholemeal spelt
   or wheat flour
1 tbsp baking powder
½ tsp fine sea salt
2 tbsp extra virgin olive oil,
   plus extra for frying

1 egg, beaten
350ml/12fl oz/scant 1½ cups rice milk,
   plus extra as needed
70g/2½oz/½ cup blueberries, chopped
   strawberries or chopped banana (optional)
butter, maple syrup, ½ lemon, sugar

1 Preheat the oven to 70°C/150°F/Gas ¼. In a small bowl, mix together the flour, baking powder and salt. In a medium bowl, whisk together the olive oil, egg and rice milk. Pour the dry mixture into the wet ingredients and whisk until smooth. Fold in the blueberries, if using.

2 Heat a griddle over a medium-low heat until hot or heat a little olive oil in a large frying pan. For each pancake, drop 1–2 tablespoonfuls of the batter onto the hot griddle, spacing them slightly apart. If the batter is too thick and the pancakes don't spread, add a little more milk 1 tablespoon at a time to thin out the batter. Cook for 2 minutes until the bubbles on the surface pop and the undersides of the pancakes are lightly browned. Flip the pancakes over and cook for another 1–2 minutes until lightly browned. Transfer to a plate and keep warm in the oven while you make the remaining pancakes. If using a frying pan, add more oil to the pan as necessary before cooking each batch.

3 Spread each pancake with a little butter and serve hot, drizzled with maple syrup or sprinkled with lemon juice and sugar.

STORAGE: Refrigerate the batter for up to 2 days. Refrigerate the cooked pancakes for up to 3 days.

HEALTH BENEFITS

SPELT is an ancient grain related to wheat. It offers a broader spectrum of nutrients, and people with wheat sensitivities can often eat it instead.

RICE MILK is an excellent substitute for cow's milk in baking. Made from brown rice, it has a lovely natural sweetness.

BLUEBERRIES are packed with antioxidant vitamins C and E. They're great for healthy cell growth and healthy cholesterol levels.

044 **Scrambled Eggs**

Protein-packed scrambled eggs are easy for small children to eat. Give your baby a spoon and she should be able to scoop them up from a bowl. The mustard gives them a flavour boost that will spark her interest.

SERVES: 2 adults and 2 children   **PREP TIME:** 5 mins   **COOK TIME:** 4 mins

30g/1oz butter

8 eggs, beaten

¼ tsp fine sea salt

1 tbsp non-hot mustard (optional)

1 Melt the butter in a large frying pan over a medium-high heat until gently sizzling. Pour the eggs into the pan and sprinkle with the salt. Cook for 1 minute until the edges of the eggs start to sizzle, then stir with a small wooden spoon for 2–3 minutes until just cooked. Remove from the heat.

2 Stir in the mustard, if using, and serve immediately.

045 **Fried Egg on Rye**

If your baby can chew, this is a good lunch. My son Nicholas loves how the egg gets a little crunchy when it's fried in the butter, and it's especially delicious with the toasted rye bread and mayonnaise.

SERVES: 2 adults and 2 children **PREP TIME:** 5 mins **COOK TIME:** 5 mins

30g/1oz butter	6 slices of wholemeal rye bread
6 eggs	mayonnaise, to taste, for spreading

1 Melt the butter in a large frying pan over a medium-high heat. When it is sizzling hot, break the eggs into the pan one at a time and gently break the yolks. Work in batches if necessary.
2 Reduce the heat to medium and cook for 5 minutes until the eggs are just cooked. Meanwhile, toast the bread.
3 Spread some mayonnaise on each slice of bread and top with 1 egg. Serve warm.

046 **Squash & Potato Soup**

This is a quick and easy soup that's perfect on a crisp autumn day. Kids love the velvety texture, bright colour and gentle sweetness.

SERVES: 2 adults and 2 children   **PREP TIME:** 15 mins   **COOK TIME:** 30 mins

1 small butternut squash, peeled, deseeded and cubed
2 potatoes, unpeeled and diced
2 onions, chopped
2 garlic cloves, roughly chopped
⅛ tsp cayenne pepper
455ml/16fl oz/scant 2 cups vegetable stock
80ml/2½fl oz/⅓ cup extra virgin olive oil

1 Put the squash, potatoes, onions, garlic, cayenne pepper and vegetable stock in a large saucepan and bring to the boil over a medium-high heat. Reduce the heat to medium-low and simmer, covered, for 30 minutes until the squash and potatoes are soft.

2 Using an immersion blender, purée the mixture for 1–2 minutes until creamy but still chunky. Add the olive oil and serve hot.

STORAGE: Refrigerate for up to 3 days or freeze for up to 3 months

047 **Creamy Rustic Soup**

This is a great soup for children because it's substantial enough to be a whole meal. It's especially good in the autumn or winter.

SERVES: 2 adults and 2 children **PREP TIME:** 25 mins, plus overnight soaking **COOK TIME:** 1¾ hours

100g/3½oz/½ cup pearl barley

55g/2oz/⅓ cup spelt grain

70g/2½oz/⅓ cup split red lentils

70g/2½oz/⅓ cup dried mung beans

1 strip of kombu, about 15 x 5cm/6 x 2in

5 tbsp extra virgin olive oil

2 onions, chopped

6 garlic cloves, quartered

2 carrots, quartered lengthways and sliced

2 large tomatoes, chopped

3 tbsp vegetable bouillon powder

Tabasco sauce, to serve (optional)

1 Put the barley, spelt, red lentils and mung beans in a large bowl, cover with warm water and leave to soak, covered, overnight.

2 Drain and rinse the soaked grain and bean mixture. Transfer it to a large saucepan and add 1.5l/52fl oz/6 cups water. Bring to the boil over a high heat and boil for 10 minutes, skimming any scum that rises to the surface. Reduce the heat to medium-low, add the kombu and simmer, covered, for 45 minutes until the grains and beans are soft, then discard the kombu.

3 Meanwhile, heat a small saucepan over a medium heat. Add 1 tablespoon of the olive oil and when it is hot, add the onions and garlic. Cook for 10 minutes, stirring frequently, until brown.

4 When the grain and bean mixture is cooked, add the onions and garlic along with the carrots, tomatoes and vegetable bouillon powder. Simmer, covered, over a low heat for a further 1 hour, stirring occasionally, until the vegetables are very tender.

5 Divide the soup into four bowls and drizzle each portion with 1 tablespoon of the remaining olive oil. Season the adult portions with the Tabasco sauce, if using. Serve hot.

STORAGE: Refrigerate for up to 3 days or freeze for up to 3 months.

048 **Hummus, Sprouts & Avocado**

This is a delicious reminder of why hummus is great to have in the fridge – and when you make your own, you control how much salt goes into it.

SERVES: 2 adults and 2 children   **PREP TIME:** 20 mins, plus overnight soaking   **COOK TIME:** 2¼ hours

6 slices of wholemeal spelt or wheat bread
2 avocados, halved, pitted and peeled,
   then sliced
55g/2oz alfalfa sprouts
½ lemon, cut into wedges

Hummus:
100g/3½oz/½ cup dried chickpeas
3 tbsp plus 2 tsp lemon juice
1 strip of kombu, about 8 x 5cm/3 x 2in
2 garlic cloves, crushed
1 tbsp tahini
4 tbsp extra virgin olive oil
¼ tsp fine sea salt

1 To make the hummus, put the chickpeas and 2 teaspoons of the lemon juice in a medium saucepan, cover with warm water and leave to soak, covered, overnight.

2 Drain and rinse the chickpeas. Return them to the pan and add 670ml/23fl oz/2⅔ cups water. Bring to the boil over a high heat and boil for 10 minutes, skimming any scum that rises to the surface. Reduce the heat to low, add the kombu and simmer, covered, for 2 hours until the chickpeas are soft. Remove from the heat and leave the mixture to cool completely.

3 Drain and rinse well, then put the chickpeas and kombu in a blender. Add the garlic, tahini, olive oil, salt, remaining lemon juice and 4 tablespoons water. Blend for 1–2 minutes until smooth.

4 Toast the bread and then spread 1 tablespoon of the hummus on each slice and top with a few slices of the avocado. Divide the sprouts over the avocado, then squeeze the lemon wedges over. Cut into strips and serve immediately.

STORAGE: Refrigerate the hummus for up to 3 days.

HEALTH BENEFITS

CHICKPEAS are high in fibre, which prevents spikes in blood sugar levels. Combined with grains, they are a fat-free protein, so serve them with good oils for a healthy meal.

LEMONS are an excellent source of vitamin C, which is vital for a strong immune system. When added to foods, fresh lemon juice lifts the flavour and adds zing.

SEAWEEDS are low in calories and rich in essential minerals, vitamins and protein, and important trace elements missing from land vegetables due to soil depletion.

049 **Cheese & Onion Rye Toasts**

This is a cross between an American grilled cheese sandwich and English cheese on toast. The red onion softens while the cheese melts underneath, creating a flavour and texture that your little one will find delightful.

SERVES: 2 adults and 2 children   **PREP TIME:** 10 mins   **COOK TIME:** 4 mins

6 slices of wholemeal rye bread
non-hot mustard, to taste, for spreading

175g/6oz mature Cheddar cheese, sliced
1 red onion, quartered and sliced

1 Preheat the grill to medium. Meanwhile, toast the bread in a toaster, then spread a little mustard on one side of each slice and put them on a large baking sheet. Divide the cheese over each slice, covering well, then evenly arrange the onion over the cheese.

2 Grill for 4 minutes until the onion has softened and the cheese is beginning to melt. Serve hot.

050 **Mashed Potato Craters**

A gorgeous way to eat potatoes, this dish is also fun for kids. For variation, you can substitute the olive oil with butter or gravy. A hearty mixed salad is a great accompaniment.

SERVES: 2 adults and 2 children **PREP TIME:** 15 mins **COOK TIME:** 20 mins

1kg/2lb 4oz potatoes, diced
2 carrots, diced
3 garlic cloves

½ tsp fine sea salt
4 tbsp extra virgin olive oil

1 Put the potatoes, carrots and garlic in a steamer and steam, covered, over boiling water for 20 minutes until the potatoes and carrots are soft. Remove from the heat and transfer to a medium bowl, reserving the steam water.

2 Add the salt and a little of the reserved steam water to the vegetables and blend, using an immersion blender, for 1–2 minutes until smooth and creamy. Add additional steam water if needed.

3 Using a tablespoon, divide the mixture onto four plates, mounding each portion up into a mountain. The two adult portions should be twice as big as the two child portions. Using a teaspoon, hollow a crater into the top of each mountain. Pour 4 teaspoons of the olive oil into each of the adult portions and 2 teaspoons into the child portions. Serve immediately.

051 No-Meat Meatballs

These succulent tofu balls are a delicious alternative to meatballs.

SERVES: 2 adults and 2 children   **PREP TIME:** 30 mins, plus making the sauce   **COOK TIME:** 35 mins

1 tbsp extra virgin olive oil

1 small onion, chopped

2 slices of wholemeal wheat or spelt bread, lightly toasted

400g/14oz firm tofu, drained

3 eggs, beaten

40g/1½oz Cheddar cheese, grated

¼ tsp salt, plus extra for cooking the pasta

1 tsp dried oregano

300g/10½oz dried spelt or wheat pasta

½ recipe quantity Tomato Sauce (see page 137), hot

1 Preheat the oven to 180°C/350°F/Gas 4 and grease a large baking dish with 1 teaspoon of the olive oil. Heat the remaining olive oil in a small frying pan over a medium-high heat, add the onion and cook for 5 minutes, stirring occasionally, until beginning to soften. Meanwhile, put the bread in a blender and blend for 1 minute until breadcrumbs form.

2 Crumble the tofu into a large bowl. Add the breadcrumbs, onion, eggs, Cheddar, salt and oregano and mix well with a fork.

3 Shape the mixture into 20 balls of equal size and put them in the prepared baking dish. Bake for 30 minutes. Meanwhile, cook the pasta according to the packet instructions, then drain and transfer to a serving bowl. Serve hot with the tomato sauce and no-meat meatballs.

STORAGE: Refrigerate for up to 3 days.

052 **Polenta with Shiitake Mushrooms**

Polenta is wonderfully versatile, and children love its subtle, sweet flavour. Try mixing in extra ingredients, such as six whole garlic cloves, a chopped onion, and/or grated cheese, in step 1.

SERVES: 2 adults and 2 children **PREP TIME:** 15 mins **COOK TIME:** 45 mins

30g/1oz butter, plus extra for greasing
175g/6oz/1 cup polenta
1 tsp fine sea salt
1 onion, finely chopped
1 garlic clove, finely chopped

1 tsp dried thyme
450g/1lb shiitake mushrooms, brushed
    clean, stems discarded and caps sliced
185ml/6fl oz/¾ cup Greek yogurt

1 Grease a 30cm/12in round baking dish with butter and set aside. Put 875ml/30fl oz/3½ cups water in a heavy-based saucepan and bring to the boil over a high heat. Pour in the polenta, whisking continuously with a metal whisk until smooth. Stir in the salt and reduce the heat to low. Cook for 15 minutes, stirring continuously, until the polenta is thick and rubbery, then pour it into the baking dish and smooth the top using a rubber spatula. Leave to cool and set.

2 While the polenta is cooling, make the mushroom mixture. Melt the butter in a large frying pan over a medium-high heat. Add the onion and cook for 5 minutes, stirring, until lightly browned. Add the garlic and thyme and continue cooking for a further 3 minutes, stirring occasionally.

3 Increase the heat to high and add the mushrooms. Cook for 10 minutes, stirring continuously, until the mushrooms are golden brown. Remove from the heat and stir in the yogurt, then set aside.

4 Preheat the grill to medium. Cut the polenta into 8 wedges and grill in the baking dish for 5 minutes until warm and crisp.

5 Divide the grilled polenta onto 4 plates and spoon 2 tablespoons of the mushroom mixture over the top of each portion. Serve immediately.

STORAGE: Refrigerate the polenta and mushrooms separately for up to 3 days.

053 Sweetcorn & Pea Pancakes

These simple, savoury pancakes are a great way to get your child to eat his peas. They're good on their own, but for variation try them served with yogurt on the side or with grated cheese sprinkled on top.

SERVES: 2 adults and 2 children **PREP TIME**: 10 mins **COOK TIME**: 20 mins

125g/4½oz/1 cup wholemeal spelt
   or wheat flour
1 tsp baking powder
2 eggs, beaten
150ml/5fl oz/scant ⅔ cup milk

85g/3oz/¾ cup peas
85g/3oz/¾ cup sweetcorn
½ tsp fine sea salt
1 tsp extra virgin olive oil

1 Preheat the oven to 70°C/150°F/Gas ¼. Put the flour and baking powder in a medium bowl and mix well. Whisk in the eggs and milk until smooth and then stir in the peas, sweetcorn and salt.

2 Heat the olive oil in a large frying pan over a medium-low heat. Pour tablespoonfuls of the batter into the pan, spacing well apart, and cook for 2–3 minutes on each side until lightly browned. Alternatively, cook the pancakes on a griddle over a medium-low heat for 2–3 minutes on each side until lightly browned. Transfer to a plate and keep warm in the oven while you make the remaining pancakes. Serve hot.

STORAGE: Refrigerate the cooked pancakes for up to 3 days.

054 **Baked Frittata**

A frittata is a type of Italian omelette that often includes meats, cheeses and vegetables.

SERVES: 2 adults and 2 children   **PREP TIME:** 15 mins   **COOK TIME:** 55 mins

butter, for greasing
350g/12oz red potatoes,
   unpeeled and diced
2 tsp extra virgin olive oil
1 onion, chopped
5 eggs, beaten

120g/4¼oz frozen spinach, chopped
175g/6oz feta cheese, diced
55g/2oz/½ cup pitted Kalamata olives,
   cut into rings
Tabasco sauce (optional), to serve

1 Preheat the oven to 200°C/400°F/Gas 6 and generously grease a large pie plate or round baking dish with butter. Bring a large saucepan of water to the boil and cook the potatoes for 10 minutes until soft. Remove from the heat, drain and leave to cool.

2 Heat the oil in a medium frying pan over a medium heat. Add the onion and cook for 10 minutes, stirring occasionally, until brown. Stir in the potatoes, eggs, spinach, feta and olives and mix well, then pour the mixture into the prepared baking dish. Bake for 25–30 minutes until the egg is just cooked. Meanwhile, preheat the grill to medium.

3 Transfer the baking dish to the top shelf under the grill and grill for 3 minutes until the cheese is lightly browned. Serve hot with the Tabasco sauce, if using.

STORAGE: Refrigerate for up to 3 days.

055 Roasted Veggies with Feta

The roasted garlic combined with rosemary and feta cheese in this dish makes a fabulous mix. Children love the colourful vegetables, which are sweet and delicious when roasted.

SERVES: 2 adults and 2 children   **PREP TIME:** 20 mins   **COOK TIME:** 25 mins

4 tbsp extra virgin olive oil
375g/13oz potatoes, diced
1 carrot, quartered lengthways and sliced
10 garlic cloves
½ tsp dried rosemary

100g/3½oz broccoli,
    cut into bite-sized florets
1 small red pepper, deseeded
    and finely diced
175g/6oz feta cheese, diced

1 Preheat the oven to 230°C/450°F/Gas 8 and grease a medium baking dish with 1 tablespoon of the olive oil. Put the potatoes, carrot, garlic, rosemary and 2 tablespoons of the remaining olive oil in a large bowl and mix well, then pour the mixture into the baking dish. Bake for 15 minutes until the vegetables are beginning to soften.

2 Meanwhile, put the broccoli, red pepper, feta cheese and the remaining olive oil in another bowl and mix well.

3 Remove the vegetables from the oven and stir in the broccoli mixture. Bake for a further 10 minutes until the vegetables and feta are beginning to brown. Serve hot.

STORAGE: Refrigerate for up to 3 days.

056 **Kamut Pasta with Veggies & Walnuts**

Walnuts are super-rich in good quality oil. Toasting the walnuts makes all the difference in flavour in this delicious pasta dish that my children love.

SERVES: 2 adults and 2 children **PREP TIME:** 30 mins **COOK TIME:** 25 mins

½ tsp fine sea salt,
  plus extra for cooking the pasta
280g/10oz broccoli,
  cut into bite-sized florets
100g/3½oz/1 cup walnut halves, chopped
250g/9oz/3 cups dried Kamut pasta

135ml/4½fl oz/½ cup plus 2 tsp
  extra virgin olive oil
1 onion, chopped
3 garlic cloves, chopped
10 basil leaves, torn

1 Preheat the grill to medium and bring a large pan of salted water to the boil. Put the broccoli in a steamer and steam, covered, over boiling water for 5 minutes until just soft. Meanwhile, put the walnuts on a small baking tray and grill for 4–5 minutes until just beginning to brown. Remove from the heat and leave to cool.

2 Cook the pasta according to the packet instructions. Meanwhile, heat 2 teaspoons of the olive oil in a medium frying pan over a medium heat. Add the onion and cook for 8 minutes, stirring, until lightly browned. Add the garlic and cook for a further 2 minutes.

3 When the pasta has finished cooking, drain it and transfer to a large bowl. Add the onion mixture, broccoli, walnuts, basil, salt and remaining olive oil and mix well. Serve warm.

057 Arame Rice with Toasted Seeds

Seaweed is the perfect way to add not only extra flavour but extra goodness, too. Toasted seeds make any dish more interesting because their roasted flavour is so good.

SERVES: 2 adults and 2 children   **PREP TIME:** 10 mins, plus overnight soaking   **COOK TIME:** 30 mins

175g/6oz/1 cup brown basmati rice
1 tbsp natural yogurt or kefir
5g/⅛oz/2 tbsp arame
2 tbsp sunflower seeds, pulsed in a blender

2 tbsp pumpkin seeds, pulsed in a blender
1 tsp tamari soy sauce
4 tbsp extra virgin olive oil

1 Put the rice, yogurt and 500ml/17fl oz/2 cups warm water in a medium saucepan and leave to soak, covered, for at least 7 hours or overnight.

2 Bring the rice to the boil over a high heat, then reduce the heat to low and simmer, covered, for 30 minutes until the rice is just tender.

3 Meanwhile, crumble the arame into a bowl, using your hands or a pestle and mortar, and cover with boiled water. Leave to soak for 15 minutes, then drain. Heat a medium frying pan over a medium heat. When it is hot, add the sunflower and pumpkin seeds and the tamari and cook for 3–4 minutes, stirring with a wooden spoon, until lightly toasted and dry.

4 Transfer the seeds to a serving bowl and add the rice, arame and olive oil. Mix well and serve warm or at room temperature.

STORAGE: Refrigerate for up to 1 day. Reheat until hot.

058 Lemon Mackerel & Cucumber Sandwiches

This is great for lunch – or lunchboxes when your child is older. The lemon juice adds freshness to the oily fish and the cucumber adds crunch.

SERVES: 2 adults and 2 children   **PREP TIME:** 10 mins

250g/9oz smoked mackerel

4 tbsp mayonnaise, plus extra for spreading

2 tbsp lemon juice

8 slices of wholemeal wheat bread

16 cucumber rounds

1 Remove and discard the skin from the mackerel and remove any bones, feeling the flesh with your fingers. Shred the mackerel into a small bowl with a fork. Add the mayonnaise and lemon juice and mix well.

2 Spread each slice of bread with a little mayonnaise. Evenly divide the cucumber rounds onto four slices of the bread and spread the mackerel on top of them. Cover with the remaining slices of bread, cut each sandwich diagonally into two triangles and serve.

STORAGE: Refrigerate the mackerel mixture for up to 2 days.

059 Chicken & Mushroom Pasta

Adding raw, grated vegetables to a dish is a great way to increase your child's intake of vitamins and minerals. They also add freshness and flavour.

SERVES: 2 adults and 2 children   **PREP TIME**: 15 mins   **COOK TIME**: 25 mins

55g/2oz butter
400g/14oz boneless, skinless chicken breast
225g/8oz/3 cups dried wholemeal spelt
   or wheat pasta shells

100g/3½oz button mushrooms, chopped
1 small carrot, grated
2 tbsp extra virgin olive oil
fine sea salt

1 Melt half of the butter in a small frying pan over a medium-high heat. Season both sides of the chicken with salt and add it to the pan. Cook, covered, for 5 minutes on each side until cooked through and the juices run clear. Transfer the chicken to a plate and leave to cool, then cut it into bite-sized pieces.
2 Bring a large saucepan of salted water to the boil and cook the pasta according to the packet instructions, then drain and transfer to a serving bowl.
3 Meanwhile, melt the remaining butter in the same frying pan over a medium-low heat. Add the mushrooms and fry for 10 minutes, stirring occasionally, until lightly browned.
4 Add the chicken, mushrooms, carrot and olive oil to the pasta and toss well. Serve warm.

STORAGE: Refrigerate for up to 2 days.

060 **Best Beef Burgers**

My dad loved beef burgers when I was growing up – thrown on the barbecue from spring to autumn and cooked inside in the winter. The chopped onion transforms ordinary burgers into a wonderful treat.

SERVES: 2 adults and 2 children   **PREP TIME:** 10 mins   **COOK TIME:** 10 mins

450g/1lb beef mince

1 small onion, finely chopped

1 tbsp extra virgin olive oil

fine sea salt and freshly ground
    black pepper

To serve (optional):

3 wholemeal spelt or wheat hamburger buns

lettuce

sliced tomato

sliced gherkins

1 Put the mince and onion in a medium bowl and mix well. Shape some of the mixture into 4 small patties, about 5cm/2in wide and 2cm/¾in high, for child portions. Shape the remaining mixture into 2 patties, about 9cm/3½in wide and 2cm/¾in high, for adult portions. Season with salt and pepper and put the patties on a plate.

2 Heat the olive oil in a large frying pan over a medium-high heat and put the burgers in the pan. Fry, partially covered, for 4–5 minutes on each side until crispy and brown. Serve hot. Adults may enjoy this on a wholemeal bun with lettuce, tomato and gherkin, while little mouths will need theirs served with one-quarter or one-half of a bun and the vegetables, if desired.

STORAGE: Refrigerate uncooked burgers for up to 2 days or freeze for up to 1 month.

Chapter 4

2–3 YEARS

When your child is old enough to feed himself and eat with the rest of the family, you can cook foods that are more sophisticated and require more coordination to eat. He'll have fun assembling Make-Your-Own Sushi and digging into the grown-up flavours found in dishes such as Prawn Pasta Bake and Curry Rice with Cranberries & Almonds. Let him help with easy tasks in the kitchen, too. This can be great fun and can spark a deeper interest in food. Your child may be little, but there's usually something to be poured, added or stirred that even little hands can manage. Plus, when a child helps to make something, he usually really wants to eat it when it's ready. He can also just sit and watch while you explain what you're doing. It's a great way to spend time together and for him to learn.

Blueberry Loaf (see page 119)

061 Chilli Non Carne

This hearty chilli features weekly on the meal planner in my house. If you want to make a meat chilli, use beef instead of the tempeh. Brown 175g/6oz beef mince in 2 tablespoons olive oil and add it to the chilli 20 minutes before it has finished cooking.

SERVES: 2 adults and 2 children   **PREP TIME:** 25 mins, plus overnight soaking   **COOK TIME:** 2¾ hours

125g/4½oz/¾ cup dried pinto beans
2 tsp lemon juice
1 strip of kombu, about 15 x 5cm/6 x 2in
1 tbsp extra virgin olive oil
1 large onion, chopped
2 garlic cloves, crushed
175g/6oz tempeh, cut into small cubes

1 orange pepper, deseeded and chopped
480g/1lb 1oz/3⅓ cups chopped tinned
   tomatoes
¼ tsp chilli powder, or to taste
¾ tsp fine sea salt
175g/6oz mature Cheddar cheese, grated
low-salt corn chips (optional), to serve

1 Put the beans and lemon juice in a medium saucepan, cover with warm water and leave to soak, covered, overnight.

2 Drain and rinse the beans. Return them to the pan and add 570ml/20fl oz/scant 2⅓ cups water. Bring to the boil over a high heat and boil for 10 minutes, skimming any scum that rises. Reduce the heat to low, add the kombu and simmer, covered, for 2 hours until soft.

3 Meanwhile, heat the olive oil in a large saucepan over a medium-low heat. Add the onion and cook for 8 minutes, stirring continuously, until lightly browned. Add the garlic and cook, stirring, for a further 2 minutes. Stir in the tempeh, pepper, tomatoes and chilli powder.

4 Mash together the beans, kombu and cooking liquid and add to the tempeh mixture. Cook, covered, for 1 hour, stirring occasionally, until well cooked and the flavours have blended.

5 Stir in the salt and sprinkle the chilli generously with the Cheddar. Serve by itself or with corn chips, if you like.

STORAGE: Refrigerate vegetarian chilli for up to 3 days and beef chilli for up to 2 days.

062 Baked Artichoke Hearts

We love artichokes any which way, but combining them with crunchy roasted garlic and zingy lemon zest makes this beautiful dish divine. This is my daughter Jess' favourite meal.

SERVES: 2 adults and 2 children **PREP TIME:** 15 mins **COOK TIME:** 30 mins

115ml/3¾fl oz/scant ½ cup extra virgin
    olive oil, plus extra for greasing
1 slice of wholemeal wheat bread
    or 30g/1oz/½ cup breadcrumbs
50g/1¾oz/½ cup grated Parmesan cheese
4 garlic cloves, finely chopped

1 tbsp chopped parsley
juice and zest of ½ lemon
950g/2lb 2oz tinned artichoke hearts
    in water, drained, squeezed and halved
    lengthways

1 Preheat the oven to 180°C/350°F/Gas 4 and grease a 23cm/9in round baking dish with olive oil. If using fresh bread, lightly toast it and then put it in a blender. Blend for 1 minute until breadcrumbs form. Put the breadcrumbs in a small bowl and mix in the olive oil, Parmesan, garlic, parsley and lemon juice and zest.

2 Top each artichoke half with 1 teaspoon of the breadcrumb mixture and put the artichokes mixture-side up in the prepared baking dish.

3 Sprinkle any remaining breadcrumb mixture in the baking dish and bake for 30 minutes until golden brown. Serve hot.

STORAGE: Refrigerate for up to 3 days.

063 Brussels Sprout & Barley Stew

If your child has only had Brussels sprouts with butter, he must try them like this. He'll find this rich, well-flavoured stew hearty and satisfying.

SERVES: 2 adults and 2 children   **PREP TIME:** 30 mins, plus overnight soaking   **COOK TIME:** 1½ hours

100g/3½oz/½ cup pearl barley
½ tbsp natural yogurt or kefir
½ tbsp extra virgin olive oil
1 small onion, chopped
2 tomatoes, halved

175g/6oz Brussels sprouts, trimmed
and quartered lengthways
1½ tbsp tamari
½ tbsp vegetarian Worcestershire sauce

1 Put the barley and yogurt in a large bowl, cover with warm water and leave to soak, covered, for at least 7 hours or overnight, then drain.

2 Put the barley and 700ml/24fl oz/generous 2¾ cups water in a very large saucepan and bring to the boil over a high heat. Reduce the heat to low and simmer, covered, for 45 minutes.

3 Meanwhile, heat the olive oil in a small saucepan over a medium-high heat. Add the onion and cook for 10 minutes, stirring occasionally, until soft and slightly browned. Make a triangular cut at the stem-end of each tomato half to remove the hard part, then chop the tomatoes.

4 Add the onion, tomatoes, Brussels sprouts, tamari and Worcestershire sauce to the barley and simmer, covered, for a further 45 minutes until the barley is soft. Serve hot.

STORAGE: Refrigerate for up to 3 days or freeze for up to 3 months.

064 **Baked Mushroom Open Sandwich**

With crunchy bread and melting cheese, these excellently flavoured warm sandwiches make a fabulous meal.

SERVES: 2 adults and 2 children   **PREP TIME:** 30 mins, plus 1 hour chilling   **COOK TIME:** 40 mins

2 tbsp plus 2 tsp extra virgin olive oil

1 small onion, finely chopped

115g/4oz button mushrooms,
   brushed clean and chopped

55g/2oz/½ cup pitted black olives,
   cut into rings

115g/4oz mature Cheddar cheese, grated

2 garlic cloves, chopped

1 tsp dried oregano

320ml/11fl oz/scant 1⅓ cups Tomato Sauce
   (see page 137)

1 large wholemeal wheat bloomer,
   cut in half lengthways

1 Heat 2 teaspoons of the olive oil in a small frying pan over a medium heat. Add the onion and cook for 10 minutes, stirring occasionally, until soft. Remove from the heat.

2 Put the mushrooms, olives, Cheddar, garlic, remaining olive oil and oregano in a medium bowl. Add the onion and the tomato sauce and toss well. Cover and chill for at least 1 hour.

3 Preheat the oven to 180°C/350°F/Gas 4. Remove some of the crumb from the centre of each piece of bread to create a shallow hollow, then put the bread crust-side down on a baking sheet. Spread each half generously with the mushroom sauce. Bake for 30 minutes until the cheese has melted, then slice and serve hot.

STORAGE: Refrigerate any leftover sauce for up to 3 days or freeze in portion-sized jars for up to 3 months.

065 Toasted Quinoa & Vegetable Salad

This colourful, nutrient-packed salad is perfect for kids – and it's incredibly versatile: you can use any combination of finely chopped vegetables to cater to your child's growing tastes.

SERVES: 2 adults and 2 children   **PREP TIME:** 20 mins   **COOK TIME:** 35 mins

85g/3oz/½ cup quinoa
75g/2½oz broccoli, cut into tiny florets
juice of ½ lemon
1 tbsp extra virgin olive oil
1 tbsp tahini
1 carrot, grated

½ yellow pepper, deseeded
  and finely chopped
140g/5oz cucumber, finely chopped
4 small spring onions, thinly sliced
30g/1oz alfalfa sprouts

1 Put the quinoa in a sieve and rinse under cold running water, then drain well. Transfer to a medium saucepan and toast over a high heat for 5 minutes, stirring continuously, until any excess water has evaporated and the quinoa has browned slightly and begun to pop.

2 Slowly add 375ml/13fl oz/1½ cups water and bring to the boil over a high heat. Reduce the heat to low and simmer, covered, for 30 minutes until tender. Remove from the heat and leave to cool.

3 Shortly before the quinoa has finished cooking, put the broccoli in a steamer and steam, covered, over boiling water for 3 minutes until tender. Meanwhile, put the lemon juice, olive oil and tahini in a small bowl and mix well, then set aside.

4 Transfer the broccoli to a bowl and add the quinoa, carrot, yellow pepper, cucumber, spring onions and alfalfa sprouts and toss together. Pour the dressing over, mix well and serve.

STORAGE: Refrigerate for up to 3 days, but don't reheat. Serve cold or at room temperature.

HEALTH BENEFITS

QUINOA is a complete protein, with all the essential amino acids your child needs, including cystine, lysine and methionine – which are low in other grains.

TAHINI is rich in essential oils that support brain and nerve development, iron and B vitamins for healthy cell growth, and methionine to keep the liver healthy.

SPROUTS are rich in vitamins, minerals and proteins. These nutritious 'live foods' are buzzing with live enzymes, which boost the digestive system.

066 Potato & Parsnip Pancakes

This delicious twist on the classic potato pancake is a good way to incorporate parsnip into a new favourite for your little one.

SERVES: 2 adults and 2 children   **PREP TIME:** 10 mins   **COOK TIME:** 18 mins

3 eggs
85g/3oz/1 cup grated parsnip
140g/5oz/1 cup grated potato

5 tbsp wholemeal spelt or wheat flour
30g/1oz butter

1 Put the eggs in a medium bowl and beat with a wire whisk, then mix in the parsnip, potato and flour until blended.

2 Preheat the oven to 70°C/150°F/Gas ¼. Melt the butter in a large frying pan over a medium-low heat, then drop tablespoonfuls of the parsnip mixture into the pan, spacing them well apart and flattening to 1cm/½in thick. Fry for 3 minutes on each side until lightly browned and cooked through. Transfer to a plate and keep warm in the oven while you make the remaining pancakes. Serve warm.

067 Pecan & Stilton Stuffed Mushrooms

If your child likes stuffed mushrooms, he'll absolutely love these. Serve them with a big mixed salad and some fresh wholemeal bread for a deliciously satisfying meal.

SERVES: 2 adults and 2 children   PREP TIME: 15 mins   COOK TIME: 30 mins

6 large, flat field mushrooms (the larger and flatter, the better), brushed clean
30g/1oz butter
1 large onion, finely chopped
30g/1oz/¼ cup pecan halves, broken in half lengthways (check for shell fragments)

2 slices of wholemeal spelt or wheat bread
175g/6oz Stilton cheese, crumbled
1 egg, beaten
4 tbsp chopped parsley
1 lemon, cut into 6 wedges

1 Preheat the grill to medium. Carefully remove the stems from the mushrooms. Set the caps aside and finely chop the stems. Melt the butter in a medium frying pan over a medium-high heat, add the mushroom stems and onion and cook for 10 minutes, stirring occasionally, until the onion is just soft.

2 Meanwhile, put the pecans in a baking dish and grill for 2–3 minutes until lightly browned. Remove from the grill and set aside.

3 Preheat the oven to 180°C/350°F/Gas 4. Lightly toast the bread and put it in a blender. Blend for 1 minute until breadcrumbs form, then stir the breadcrumbs, pecans, Stilton, egg and parsley into the onion mixture.

4 Put the mushroom caps rounded-side down on a large baking sheet and spoon the stuffing onto each one, dividing it equally among the six mushrooms. Bake for 20 minutes until the mushrooms are cooked and sizzling and the filling is lightly browned. Squeeze the lemon wedges over the mushrooms, and serve.

068 **Mediterranean Wholewheat Fusilli**

The vegetables in this recipe are cooked until they are soft and soupy, which is ideal when you're introducing your child to aubergine.

SERVES: 2 adults and 2 children **PREP TIME:** 15 mins, plus 1 hour resting **COOK TIME:** 35 mins

200g/7oz aubergine, peeled and diced

1 tsp fine sea salt,
   plus extra for cooking the pasta

3 tbsp extra virgin olive oil,
   plus extra for drizzling

1 large onion, chopped

200g/7oz courgettes, finely diced

200g/7oz tomatoes, finely diced

3 garlic cloves, crushed

185ml/6fl oz/¾ cup vegetable stock

300g/10½oz dried wholewheat fusilli
   (spiral pasta)

¼–½ tsp cayenne pepper (optional)

1 Put the aubergine in a colander, sprinkle with the salt and leave to rest in the sink for 1 hour.

2 Heat the olive oil in a large frying pan over a medium heat. Add the onion and cook for 5 minutes, stirring occasionally, until beginning to soften. Reduce the heat to medium-low and add the aubergine, courgettes, tomatoes, garlic and vegetable stock. Continue cooking, covered, at a gentle simmer for 30 minutes, stirring occasionally, until the vegetables are cooked.

3 When the vegetables have almost finished cooking, bring a large pan of salted water to the boil and cook the pasta according to the packet instructions, then drain and return it to the pan.

4 Drizzle the pasta with a little olive oil and toss well, then divide it into four bowls. Spoon several tablespoons of the vegetable mixture over each child portion. Mix the cayenne pepper, if using, into the remaining vegetables and spoon them over the adult portions. Serve immediately.

STORAGE: Refrigerate for up to 3 days.

069 Curry Rice with Cranberries & Almonds

Here's a way to introduce tart cranberries to your child in a savoury dish. It also includes almonds, one of the healthiest nuts, which provide protein and good-quality fat. Here, they're toasted to add a nutty crunchiness.

SERVES: 2 adults and 2 children   **PREP TIME:** 10 mins, plus overnight soaking   **COOK TIME:** 35 mins

175g/6oz/1 cup brown basmati rice

1 tbsp natural yogurt or kefir

40g/1½oz/⅓ cup dried cranberries

1 tbsp extra virgin olive oil

1 small onion, finely chopped

75g/2½oz/½ cup whole almonds with skins

1 tbsp curry powder

⅛ tsp cayenne pepper

1   Put the rice, yogurt and 500ml/17fl oz/2 cups warm water in a medium saucepan and leave to soak, covered, for at least 7 hours or overnight.

2   Bring the rice to the boil over a high heat, then reduce the heat to low and simmer, covered, for 35 minutes until the rice is just tender.

3   While the rice is cooking, put the cranberries in a small bowl, cover with 4 tablespoons warm water and leave to soak for 15 minutes, then drain.

4   Meanwhile, preheat the grill to medium. Heat the olive oil in a small frying pan over a medium heat until hot. Add the onion and cook for 10 minutes, stirring occasionally, until soft.

5   Put the almonds on a baking sheet and grill for 3 minutes until lightly browned.

6   Put the rice, cranberries, onion, almonds, curry powder and cayenne pepper in a medium bowl and toss well. Serve warm.

STORAGE: Refrigerate for up to 1 day. Reheat until hot.

070 **Make-Your-Own Sushi**

Prepare the rice and vegetables, put it all on the table and you're done! Letting kids assemble their own sushi gets them involved with their food – and makes them feel grown up.

SERVES: 2 adults and 2 children   **PREP TIME:** 15 mins, plus overnight soaking   **COOK TIME:** 40 mins

175g/6oz/1 cup brown basmati rice

1 tbsp natural yogurt or kefir

1 small piece horseradish root, peeled and finely grated, or 3–4 tbsp bottled horseradish sauce

3–4 tbsp mayonnaise, plus extra as needed (optional)

12 sheets of nori, cut in half crossways

1 cucumber, cut into thin matchsticks

2 carrots, cut into thin matchsticks

1 avocado, halved, pitted and peeled, then cut into strips

100g/3½oz alfalfa sprouts

umeboshi paste

wasabi paste

1 Put the rice, yogurt and 500ml/17fl oz/2 cups warm water in a medium saucepan and leave to soak, covered, for at least 7 hours or overnight.

2 Bring the rice to the boil, reduce the heat to low and cook, covered, for 40 minutes until tender.

3 Meanwhile, divide the grated horseradish root, if using, into two small bowls and mix with the mayonnaise. For adults, use equal amounts; for children use 1 part horseradish to 3 parts mayonnaise. Put the sauce on the table.

4 Set the other components of the sushi on the table: put the nori sheets on a plate and the cucumber, carrots and avocado on another. Put the sprouts, umeboshi paste, wasabi paste and rice into serving bowls.

5 Show everyone how to assemble their own sushi. Put 1 piece of nori, shiny-side down, on a plate. Spread a very thin strip of the umeboshi and wasabi pastes along the bottom of the nori, then some of the horseradish sauce, followed by 2 tablespoons of the rice. Top with vegetables and sprouts, then roll the sushi to form a log. Eat immediately.

071 Noodles with Vegetables

Miso, a fermented soya paste, is one of the world's most medicinal foods. Keep some
in the fridge and get in the habit of adding it to soups and sauces.

SERVES: 2 adults and 2 children   **PREP TIME:** 15 mins   **COOK TIME:** 10 mins

300g/10½oz udon noodles

200g/7oz carrots, cut into matchsticks

200g/7oz courgettes, cut into matchsticks

4 tbsp mellow brown miso

3 tbsp tahini

2 tbsp brown rice vinegar

1 tbsp mirin

1 garlic clove, chopped

4 spring onions, thinly sliced, to serve

fine sea salt

1 Bring a large saucepan of salted water to the boil and cook the udon noodles according to the
packet instructions, then drain.

2 While the noodles are cooking, put the carrots in a steamer and steam, covered, over boiling
water for 2 minutes. Add the courgettes and steam for a further 4 minutes until just soft.

3 Put the miso and tahini in a small saucepan and stir over a low heat until smooth. Add
80ml/2½fl oz/⅓ cup water and stir until smooth. Add the brown rice vinegar, mirin and garlic
and heat until warmed through.

4 Divide the noodles into four bowls and divide the steamed vegetables over the noodles. Top
each bowl with about 4 tablespoons of the sauce. Sprinkle with the spring onions and serve.

072 Potato Egg Salad

This fantastic potato salad, livened up by vinegar and crisp vegetables, is excellent freshly made and warm – or chilled and taken on a picnic.

SERVES: 2 adults and 2 children   **PREP TIME:** 15 mins   **COOK TIME:** 15 mins

550g/1lb 4oz potatoes, unpeeled,
  cut into large dice
4 eggs, at room temperature
1 small onion, finely chopped
2 garlic cloves, finely chopped

1 red pepper, deseeded and chopped
2 celery sticks, chopped
125ml/4fl oz/½ cup mayonnaise
4 tbsp white wine vinegar

1 Put the potatoes in steamer and steam, covered, over boiling water for 15 minutes until just soft. Remove from the heat and leave to cool.

2 Meanwhile, pierce the large end of each egg with a pin. Bring a medium saucepan of water to the boil and, using a spoon, carefully put the eggs in the water. Boil for 9 minutes, then remove from the heat, drain the hot water from the pan and refill it with cold water to cool the eggs and stop them cooking. Set aside until cool enough to handle, then drain. Peel the eggs, then quarter them lengthways and slice into bite-sized chunks.

3 Put the eggs in a large bowl and add the potatoes, onion, garlic, red pepper, celery, mayonnaise and vinegar and mix well. Serve at room temperature or chilled.

STORAGE: Refrigerate for up to 2 days.

073 Prawn Pasta Bake

I always use yogurt, a good source of calcium, protein and probiotics, instead of cream when I can because it's so much healthier, especially for little ones.

SERVES: 2 adults and 2 children   PREP TIME: 10 mins   COOK TIME: 40 mins

¼ tsp fine sea salt,
  plus extra for cooking the pasta
250g/9oz/2 cups dried wholewheat pasta,
  such as elbows or shells
300g/10½oz raw peeled prawns,
  cut into bite-sized pieces

200ml/7fl oz/scant 1 cup natural yogurt
½ tsp dried herbes de Provence
2 tbsp chopped parsley

1 Preheat the oven to 180°C/350°F/Gas 4 and bring a large saucepan of salted water to the boil. Cook the pasta for 2 minutes less than the packet instructions suggest, then remove from the heat, drain and return to the pan.

2 Mix in the prawns, yogurt, herbes de Provence, parsley and salt and transfer the mixture to a deep baking dish about 18 x 18cm/7 x 7in. Bake for 30 minutes until the prawns are completely cooked and the pasta is heated through, then serve.

STORAGE: Refrigerate for up to 2 days.

  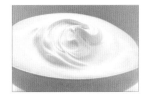

074 Hot Sardine Toasts

I could eat plain sardines until the cows come home, but if I feel like a change, this is what I crave. The creamy sauce, piquant gherkins and capers make it especially appealing to kids.

SERVES: 2 adults and 2 children   **PREP TIME:** 10 mins   **COOK TIME:** 40 mins

30g/1oz butter

1 tbsp plain flour

80ml/2½fl oz/⅓ cup mayonnaise

1 tbsp finely chopped pitted green olives

2 tbsp finely chopped gherkin

2 tbsp finely chopped onion

2 tsp small capers

½ tsp cider vinegar

6 slices of wholemeal wheat bread

350g/12oz tinned sardines, drained

1 Put the butter in the top of a double boiler or in a medium bowl resting over a pan of boiling water. Stir in the flour, then add 125ml/4fl oz/½ cup water and the mayonnaise, stirring until smooth. Continue stirring for a further 30 minutes until the mixture forms a thick sauce. Remove from the heat and mix in the olives, gherkin, onion, capers and vinegar.

2 Preheat the grill to medium. While the grill is heating, toast the bread in a toaster and put it on a baking sheet. Cover each slice of toast with the sardines. If the sardines are large, mash them onto the bread so that you have a layer of sardines. Spoon about 3 tablespoons of the sauce over the sardines and grill for 3–4 minutes until hot and the sauce is bubbling. Serve immediately.

075 Haddock with Capers

Children love this easy and delicious baked fish. The pretty cherry tomatoes and little green capers will catch their interest. Let them squeeze their own lemon and they'll like it even more.

SERVES: 2 adults and 2 children   **PREP TIME:** 10 mins   **COOK TIME:** 20 mins

extra virgin olive oil, for greasing
400g/14oz skinned haddock fillet,
   cut into 4 pieces
4 tsp capers

4 cherry tomatoes, quartered lengthways
1 lemon, cut into 4 wedges
fine sea salt

1 Preheat the oven to 150°C/300°F/Gas 2 and grease a medium baking dish with olive oil. Put the fish pieces in the dish, sprinkle lightly with salt and put 1 teaspoon of the capers and four pieces of tomato on top of each piece.
2 Bake for 20 minutes until the fish is white. Squeeze 1 lemon wedge over each piece of fish and serve hot.

STORAGE: Refrigerate for up to 2 days.

076 Chicken with Apricot & Fennel Wild Rice

Wild rice is not technically rice: it's an aquatic cereal grass native to North America. Delicious on its own, it also makes a great stuffing.

SERVES: 2 adults and 2 children   **PREP TIME:** 15 mins, plus overnight soaking   **COOK TIME:** 40 mins

125g/4½oz/¾ cup wild rice
1 tbsp natural yogurt or kefir
5 tbsp plus 2 tsp extra virgin olive oil
4 chicken breast fillets, about
   100g/3½oz each, cut into strips

6 apricots, pitted and cubed
55g/2oz fennel, finely chopped
½ tsp fine sea salt

1 Put the rice, yogurt and 500ml/17fl oz/2 cups warm water in a medium saucepan and leave to soak, covered, for at least 7 hours or overnight.

2 Bring to the boil over a high heat, then reduce the heat to low and simmer, covered, for 40 minutes until the rice is just soft. Shortly before the rice has finished cooking, heat 2 teaspoons of the olive oil in a medium frying pan over a medium heat. Put the chicken in the pan and cook for 5 minutes on each side until lightly browned and cooked through and the juices run clear.

3 Transfer the rice to a serving bowl. Mix in the apricots, fennel, salt and remaining olive oil and serve warm with the chicken.

STORAGE: Refrigerate the rice and chicken for up to 1 day. Reheat the rice until hot.

077 **Pork with Gherkins**

We were all a bit sceptical when my mom first made this dish, and then we were surprised by how much we loved it – especially when it was reheated the next day.

SERVES: 2 adults and 2 children   **PREP TIME:** 15 mins, plus overnight soaking   **COOK TIME:** 1 hour

175g/6oz/1 cup brown basmati rice

1 tbsp natural yogurt or kefir

4 pork chops, about 900g/2lb

45g/1½oz butter

1 large onion, chopped

80ml/2½fl oz/⅓ cup red wine vinegar

1 large tomato, cubed

2 tbsp tomato purée

1 tbsp chopped parsley

½ tsp dried thyme

½ tsp dried tarragon

2 tbsp Dijon mustard

85g/3oz/½ cup sliced gherkins

fine sea salt

1 Put the rice, yogurt and 500ml/17fl oz/2 cups warm water in a medium saucepan and leave to soak, covered, for at least 7 hours or overnight.

2 Sprinkle the pork chops with salt. Melt 15g/½oz of the butter in large, heavy-based frying pan over a medium-high heat, then add the pork chops and cook for 5 minutes on each side until brown. Transfer the chops to a platter. Add the remaining butter to the frying pan and melt over a medium heat. Add the onion and cook for 5 minutes, stirring occasionally, until beginning to brown. Add half of the vinegar and simmer until most of it has evaporated. Stir in the tomato, tomato purée, parsley, thyme, tarragon and 240ml/8fl oz/scant 1 cup water, then return the chops to the pan and simmer, covered, for 45 minutes until tender.

3 Meanwhile, bring the rice to the boil over a high heat, then reduce the heat to low and cook, covered, for 35 minutes until just tender. Remove from the heat and set aside.

4 Add the mustard, gherkins and remaining vinegar to the chops and mix well. Cook, covered, for a further 10 minutes, then serve warm with the rice and sauce.

STORAGE: Refrigerate for up to 2 days. Tastes even better the day after it's made.

078 Muesli Cookies

My kids love these very nutritious, very delicious cookies. The sesame seeds add a lovely toasty flavour, while the raisins and apricots add a sweet chewiness.

MAKES: About 20 cookies   **PREP TIME:** 30 mins   **COOK TIME:** 45 mins

250g/9oz butter, softened

240ml/8fl oz/scant 1 cup brown rice syrup

1 egg

1 tsp vanilla extract

300g/10½oz/2½ cups wholemeal spelt
  or wheat flour

½ tsp baking powder

115g/4oz/1 cup porridge oats

55g/2oz/½ cup quinoa flakes

50g/1¾oz/½ cup millet flakes

75g/2½oz/½ cup sunflower seeds

30g/1oz/¼ cup sesame seeds

115g/4oz/¾ cup raisins

115g/4oz/¾ cup unsulphured dried
  apricots, finely chopped

50g/1¾oz/½ cup chocolate chips (optional)

1 Preheat the oven to 180°C/350°F/Gas 4. Put the butter, brown rice syrup, egg, vanilla extract and 125ml/4fl oz/½ cup water in a large bowl and beat using an electric mixer or by hand, for 10 minutes until creamy.

2 In a medium bowl, mix together the flour, baking powder, porridge oats, quinoa flakes, millet flakes, sunflower seeds, sesame seeds, raisins, apricots and chocolate chips, if using. Add the dry mixture to the wet mixture and stir with a wooden spoon until blended.

3 Working in batches, drop 20 teaspoonfuls of the mixture onto a baking sheet, spacing them about 2cm/¾in apart. Bake for 11 minutes until lightly browned. Remove from the oven and, using a spatula, transfer the cookies to a wire rack and leave to cool. Serve warm or at room temperature.

STORAGE: Store in an airtight container at room temperature for up to 5 days.

HEALTH BENEFITS

RAISINS are excellent for relieving constipation and reducing acidity. Antiviral, antibacterial and packed with iron, raisins aid bone and teeth health and vision.

SEEDS are high in iron, vitamin E and essential fatty acids. They hold everything needed to nourish a new plant. We should eat them regularly, not only as the occasional snack.

BROWN RICE SYRUP contains complex carbohydrates and maltose which are digested slowly, so its effect on blood sugar levels is gentler than that of simple sugars.

079 Date, Oat & Hazelnut Bars

Moist, dense and filling, these bars are great for a mid-morning or afternoon snack when your child wants something sweet. They're also easy to take out and about, so you can always have a healthy snack to hand.

MAKES: 9 bars   **PREP TIME:** 15 mins, plus soaking   **COOK TIME:** 1 hour

70g/2½oz/½ cup hazelnuts

90g/3¼oz butter, melted,
   plus extra for greasing

165g/5¾oz/1½ cups porridge oats

75g/2½oz/½ cup chopped dried dates

60ml/2fl oz/¼ cup brown rice syrup

1 egg, beaten

1 tsp vanilla extract

55g/2oz/½ cup wholemeal spelt
   or wheat flour

1 tsp cinnamon

½ tsp baking powder

1 Heat the grill to medium. Put the hazelnuts on a small baking tray and grill for 3 minutes until beginning to brown. Remove from the heat and leave to cool.

2 Preheat oven to 180°C/350°F/Gas 4 and grease a 20 x 20cm/8 x 8in baking tin with butter. Put the porridge oats and dates in a bowl, stir in 375ml/13fl oz/1½ cups warm water and leave to soak for 10 minutes. Meanwhile, put the cooled hazelnuts in a plastic bag and pound them with a rolling pin or bottle until crushed, then add them to the oats.

3 Add the brown rice syrup, butter, egg and vanilla extract to the oats and mix well.

4 In another bowl, mix together the flour, cinnamon and baking powder, then add it to the oat mixture and mix well, using a wooden spoon or rubber spatula.

5 Pour the mixture into the prepared baking tin, smoothing the top with the back of a spoon. Bake for 1 hour until lightly browned. Remove from the oven and leave to cool slightly, then cut into 9 squares. Serve warm or at room temperature.

STORAGE: Store in an airtight container at room temperature for up to 2 days or refrigerate for up to 3 days.

080 **Blueberry Loaf**

Blueberries are one of nature's wonderfoods and add nutrition to everything they're used in. Eat them raw, make a pie or bake with them. You can serve this teacake as a delicious breakfast, a great afternoon snack or a delightful dessert that children will adore.

MAKES: 1 loaf **PREP TIME:** 20 mins **COOK TIME:** 1 hour

125g/4½oz butter, softened,
  plus extra for greasing
120g/4¼oz/1 cup white spelt
  or wheat flour, plus extra for flouring
115g/4oz/½ cup sugar
2 eggs

120g/4¼oz/1 cup wholemeal spelt
  or wheat flour
1 tsp baking powder
125ml/4fl oz/½ cup rice milk
250g/9oz/2 cups blueberries

1 Preheat the oven to 180°C/350°F/Gas 4 and grease and flour a 23 x 13cm/9 x 4in loaf tin. Put the butter and sugar in a large bowl and beat, using an electric mixer, for 10 minutes until light and fluffy. Add the eggs, one at a time, beating well after each one.

2 In a medium bowl, combine the flours and baking powder. Add half of the flour mixture to the butter mixture and beat until just mixed, then add the rice milk followed by the remaining flour, beating until just blended. Fold in the blueberries and spoon the mixture into the prepared tin.

3 Bake for 1 hour 5 minutes until lightly browned, cracked in the middle and just pulling away from the sides of the tin. A cocktail stick inserted into the centre should come out clean. Remove from the oven and leave to cool in the tin on a wire rack for 15 minutes, then run a knife along the sides of the tin and turn the loaf out onto the wire rack to cool completely. Serve warm or at room temperature.

STORAGE: Store in an airtight container for up to 2 days or refrigerate for up to 3 days.

Chapter 5

4–5 YEARS

It probably seems like all you did was blink, and your baby turned into a walking, talking, independent little person with aspirations and opinions of her own. If you've followed the advice in this book, she has also developed a love of good food, so carry on giving her nutritious meals whenever you can. She is experiencing more of the world on her own now and forming friendships – some of which may last a lifetime. Playdates, picnics and parties are a great chance for her to socialize with other kids and share food. From simple dishes like Guacamole and Chickpea Pancakes to indulgent treats such as Cream Cheese & Salmon Blinis, the choices are plentiful. You'll also find great salads, sandwiches and other lunchbox ideas so you can ensure that she eats well at school, too.

Mini Pitta Pizzas (see page 134)

081 **Lemon–Cinnamon Apple Slices**

Fresh fruit is a must for a lunchbox, party or picnic, and these refreshing, ready-to-eat slices are great for little hands.

SERVES: 2 adults and 2 children   **PREP TIME:** 10 mins

3 apples, halved, cored and cut into wedges   ½ tsp cinnamon
juice of ½ lemon

1 Put the apples in a medium bowl. Sprinkle with the lemon juice and toss until well coated.
2 Sprinkle the cinnamon over the apples and toss until well coated, then serve.

STORAGE: Refrigerate for up to 1 day.

082 Adzuki Yogurt Dip

Dips are always popular with kids, and this one is a nice change from hummus. It's mild, smooth and creamy – and a pretty pink colour.

SERVES: 2 adults and 2 children   **PREP TIME:** 10 mins, plus overnight soaking   **COOK TIME:** 1¼ hours

100g/3½oz/½ cup dried adzuki beans
1 tbsp lemon juice
1 strip of kombu, about 8 x 5cm/3 x 2in
60ml/2fl oz/¼ cup Greek yogurt

½ tsp ground cumin
½ tsp fine sea salt
vegetable crudités (optional), to serve
tortilla chips (optional), to serve

1 Put the beans and 1 teaspoon of the lemon juice in a medium saucepan, cover with warm water and leave to soak, covered, overnight.

2 Drain and rinse the beans. Return them to the pan and add 375ml/13fl oz/1½ cups water. Bring to the boil over a high heat and boil for 10 minutes, skimming any scum that rises to the surface. Reduce the heat to low, add the kombu and simmer, covered, for 1 hour until the beans are soft. The beans should remain covered with water, so add extra boiled water during cooking if necessary. Drain and leave to cool.

3 Put the beans and kombu, yogurt, cumin, salt and remaining lemon juice in a blender. Blend for 1 minute until smooth, then serve with vegetable crudités or tortilla chips, if you like.

STORAGE: Refrigerate for up to 3 days.

083 Guacamole

I'm always surprised at how quickly two avocados can disappear. My daughter Jess, especially, gives this winning recipe an enthusiastic thumbs up every time.

SERVES: 2 adults and 2 children   **PREP TIME:** 15 mins

2 avocados, halved and pitted
1 tomato, finely chopped
juice of 1 lemon

¼ tsp fine sea salt
⅛ tsp Tabasco sauce
vegetable sticks (optional), to serve

1 Scoop the avocado flesh into a medium bowl and mash using a fork, leaving it a bit lumpy.
2 Add the tomato, lemon juice, salt and Tabasco and mix well. Serve chilled or at room temperature, accompanied with vegetable sticks, if you like.

STORAGE: Refrigerate for up to 3 days.

084 Egg Salad

This is the egg salad I grew up with – a wonderful variation of the classic recipe. It's a great dish for lunchboxes and picnics because it's so portable. You can eat it by itself or spread it on crackers or bread.

SERVES: 2 adults and 2 children   **PREP TIME:** 15 mins   **COOK TIME:** 9 mins

6 eggs, at room temperature
2 large gherkins, cubed
1 small red onion, finely chopped
2 garlic cloves, chopped

2 tbsp chopped parsley
4 tbsp mayonnaise
4 tbsp non-hot mustard
fine sea salt

1   Pierce the large end of each egg with a pin. Bring a medium saucepan of water to the boil and, using a spoon, carefully put the eggs in the water. Boil for 9 minutes, then remove from the heat, drain the hot water from the pan and refill it with cold water to cool the eggs and stop them cooking. Set aside until cool enough to handle.

2   Peel the eggs, put them in a medium bowl and mash with a fork or potato masher. Add the gherkins, onion, garlic, parsley, mayonnaise, mustard and a pinch of salt, and mix well. Serve at room temperature or chilled.

STORAGE: Refrigerate for up to 2 days.

085 Hemp Seed & Egg Mayo Sandwich

Hemp seeds have a subtle, nutty flavour, so your child may not even taste them – but they add excellent nutrition to a lovely sandwich.

SERVES: 2 adults and 2 children   **PREP TIME:** 10 mins   **COOK TIME:** 9 mins

6 eggs, at room temperature

6 tbsp mayonnaise, plus extra for spreading

2 tbsp shelled hemp seeds

6 slices of wholemeal rye bread

1 Pierce the large end of each egg with a pin. Bring a medium saucepan of water to the boil and, using a spoon, carefully put the eggs in the water. Boil for 9 minutes, then remove from the heat, drain the hot water from the pan and refill it with cold water to cool the eggs and stop them cooking. Leave to cool for 5 minutes.

2 Peel the eggs and put them in a small bowl. Add the mayonnaise and mash with a fork. Add the hemp seeds and mix well.

3 Spread the bread with mayonnaise. Spoon the egg mayo onto 3 of the bread slices (you may have some left over) and then cover with the remaining slices of bread. Cut the sandwiches in half and serve one half for each child and two halves for each adult.

STORAGE: To pack the sandwiches for lunchboxes, wrap them in greaseproof paper, put them in plastic bags and seal to keep them fresh. The plastic bags can be re-used many times, washing them out as necessary.

086 Cheddar & Watercress Sandwich

Mature Cheddar is wonderfully flavourful. My son Nicholas loves it matched with the mustard, mayonnaise and watercress in this recipe.

SERVES: 2 adults and 2 children   **PREP TIME:** 10 mins

6 slices of wholemeal wheat bread
non-hot mustard, for spreading
mayonnaise, for spreading

180g/6¼oz mature Cheddar cheese, sliced
3 handfuls of watercress sprigs

1 Spread 3 of the bread slices with mustard and the other 3 with mayonnaise. Divide the cheese onto three of the bread slices, top with the watercress and then cover with the remaining slices of bread.

2 Cut the sandwiches in half and serve one half for each child and two halves for each adult.

STORAGE: To pack the sandwiches for lunchboxes, wrap them in greaseproof paper, put them in plastic bags and seal to keep them fresh. The plastic bags can be re-used many times, washing them out as necessary.

087 Marinated Cauliflower

This surprisingly simple and delicious way to serve cauliflower appeals to children and adults alike. It uses brown rice vinegar, which is treasured for its mellow flavour and light sweetness.

SERVES: 2 adults and 2 children   **PREP TIME:** 10 mins, plus 20 mins marinating   **COOK TIME:** 5 mins

500g/1lb 2oz cauliflower,
  cut into bite-sized florets

4 tbsp extra virgin olive oil
2 tbsp brown rice vinegar

1 Put the cauliflower in a steamer and steam, covered, over boiling water for 5 minutes until just tender.

2 Transfer the cauliflower to a medium serving bowl and, while it's still warm, drizzle the olive oil and vinegar over. Toss well and then leave to marinate at room temperature for at least 20 minutes. Serve at room temperature.

STORAGE: Keep at room temperature in a covered bowl for up to 4 hours.

088 Cherry Tomatoes with Hummus & Capers

Most kids love tomatoes, especially sweet cherry tomatoes. These pretty bite-sized morsels can be popped into little mouths one at a time.

SERVES: 2 adults and 2 children   **PREP TIME:** 20 mins, plus making the hummus

30 cherry tomatoes, about 270g/9½oz
1 recipe quantity hummus (see page 82)

2 tbsp small capers
or 30 large caper berries

1 Cut off the tops of the tomatoes and, using a melon baller or small spoon, scoop the centre and seeds out of the tomatoes and discard.
2 Fill the tomatoes with the hummus, using a tiny spoon. Top each tomato with 4–5 tiny capers or 1 caper berry, then serve.

089 Shiitake & Garlic Romaine Salad

This gorgeous salad is full of flavours. If you're transporting it for a picnic, party or lunchbox, you can mix the dressing in a little jar and dress the salad when you're ready to eat.

SERVES: 2 adults and 2 children   **PREP TIME:** 20 mins   **COOK TIME:** 14 mins

1 romaine lettuce, washed and dried
30g/1oz butter
10–12 garlic cloves, cut lengthways
    into slivers
200g/7oz shiitake mushrooms, brushed
    clean, stems discarded, and caps sliced

3 tbsp extra virgin olive oil
1 tbsp balsamic vinegar
2 tbsp shaved Parmesan cheese
fine sea salt

1 Reserve the smaller centre leaves from the lettuce and cut the remaining leaves into strips. Put them in a large salad bowl and set aside.
2 Heat a large frying pan over a medium-high heat. Add the butter and garlic and cook for 4 minutes, stirring occasionally, until starting to brown. Add the mushrooms and continue cooking for 10 minutes, stirring continuously, until brown and crisp. Remove from the heat and leave to cool.
3 Add the mushroom mixture to the lettuce strips and sprinkle with the olive oil, balsamic vinegar and Parmesan. Season with salt and toss well. Spoon the salad onto the reserved lettuce leaves and serve.

HEALTH BENEFITS
SHIITAKE MUSHROOMS have a potent flavour and have been used medicinally by the Chinese for more than 6,000 years.

They contain an active compound called lentinan, which strengthens the immune system so it can fight infection and disease.

090 **Rocket & Lemon Salad**

Rocket with lemon juice is divine. Because you're not adding oil, the leaves will still be fresh and crisp at lunchtime, making this recipe ideal for lunchboxes.

SERVES: 2 adults and 2 children   **PREP TIME:** 5 mins

6 handfuls of rocket leaves,
  roughly chopped

1 lemon, cut into wedges

1 Put the rocket in a bowl and squeeze the lemon juice over. Mix well and serve.

STORAGE: For packed lunches, transfer into airtight containers and seal.

 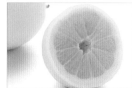

091 **Carrot & Pea Salad**

This salad is lovely and fresh and perfect for lunchboxes, and the balsamic vinegar gives it a gentle sweetness. The sweet bright green peas will really brighten up your child's meal.

SERVES: 2 adults and 2 children   **PREP TIME:** 5 mins

3 carrots, grated   2 tbsp balsamic vinegar
115g/4oz/¾ cup frozen peas, thawed

1 Put the carrots, peas and vinegar in a bowl and mix well. Serve.

STORAGE: For packed lunches you can add the peas frozen, and they will defrost by lunchtime. Transfer into airtight containers and seal.

092 **Mini Pitta Pizzas**

It's hard to go wrong with pizza – for parties or any time.

SERVES: 2 adults and 2 children   **PREP TIME:** 10 mins, plus making the sauce   **COOK TIME:** 5 mins

12 mini wholemeal pitta breads
120g/4½oz goat's cheese
170ml/5½fl oz/⅔ cup Tomato Sauce
  (see page 137)
120g/4¼oz mozzarella cheese, cubed
1 tsp dried oregano

Basil Pesto:
4 tbsp pine nuts
120g/4¼oz/2 cups tightly packed
  basil leaves
2 garlic cloves, chopped
8 tbsp grated Parmesan cheese
4 tbsp extra virgin olive oil
1 tsp fine sea salt

1 Preheat the grill to medium. Put the pine nuts for the pesto in a frying pan and heat over a medium-low heat, stirring continuously, until lightly toasted, then set aside to cool. Put the pitta breads on a baking sheet and lightly toast under the grill until they puff up and are lightly browned. Carefully cut them in half by slicing around the edge of each pitta with a sharp knife to produce 2 circles from each pitta.

2 To make the pesto, put the pine nuts, basil, garlic, Parmesan, olive oil and salt in a food processor and process for 1–2 minutes until the mixture forms a thick paste.

3 Spread 1 teaspoon of the pesto over 12 of the pitta circles, then crumble the goat's cheese over the pesto. Spread 1 tablespoon of the tomato sauce over each of the remaining 12 pitta circles and divide the mozzarella over the sauce. Put the pittas on the baking sheet, sprinkle sparingly with the oregano and grill for 2 minutes until crunchy and the cheese has melted. Serve hot.

093 **Chickpea Pancakes**

Finger foods are great at parties and these are perfect for little fingers, or for a light lunch with vegetables or salad. They have a nice flavour without being too strong.

SERVES: 2 adults and 2 children   **PREP TIME:** 10 mins, plus overnight soaking   **COOK TIME:** 2½ hours

115g/4oz/½ cup dried chickpeas	wholemeal spelt or wheat flour, as needed
2 tsp lemon juice	1 tsp ground cumin
1 strip of kombu, about 8 x 5cm/3 x 2in	½ tsp fine sea salt

1 Put the chickpeas and lemon juice in a medium saucepan, cover with warm water and leave to soak, covered, overnight.

2 Drain and rinse the chickpeas. Return them to the pan and add 455ml/16fl oz/scant 2 cups water. Bring to the boil over a high heat and boil for 10 minutes, skimming any scum that rises to the surface. Reduce the heat to low, add the kombu and simmer, covered, for 2 hours until the chickpeas are soft. Remove from the heat and drain. If using a blender with a plastic container, leave the chickpeas and kombu to cool completely before blending.

3 Transfer the chickpeas and kombu to a blender and blend for 1 minute until smooth, adding just enough fresh water to form a thick mixture. If you add too much water and the mixture is runny, add a little flour, 1 tablespoon at a time, until it thickens. Transfer the mixture to a bowl and stir in the cumin and salt.

4 Heat a griddle over a medium heat. Working in batches if necessary, drop teaspoonfuls of the chickpea mixture onto the griddle. They will spread a little and should be about 3cm/1¼in in diameter. Cook for 2–3 minutes until bubbles have popped on the surface and the undersides of the pancakes are lightly browned. Flip over and cook for a further 2–3 minutes until lightly browned. Serve hot or warm.

STORAGE: Refrigerate the cooked pancakes for up to 3 days.

094 **Parsley Pesto Penne**

Pesto, with its toasty pine nuts, fresh herbs, pungent garlic and quality olive oil, is heaven with pasta. This recipe uses parsley instead of basil and is made without cheese.

SERVES: 2 adults and 2 children   **PREP TIME:** 15 mins   **COOK TIME:** 10 mins

40g/1½oz/¼ cup pine nuts
300g/10½oz dried wholewheat penne pasta
55g/2oz/1⅓ cups chopped parsley
2 garlic cloves, crushed

½ tsp fine sea salt,
   plus extra for cooking the pasta
80ml/2½fl oz/⅓ cup extra virgin olive oil

1 Preheat the grill to medium. Put the pine nuts on a baking sheet and grill for 1 minute until toasted, watching carefully so they do not burn. Remove from the grill and set aside.
2 Bring a large saucepan of salted water to the boil. Add the pasta and cook according to the packet instructions, then drain and transfer to a large bowl.
3 While the pasta is cooking, put the pine nuts, parsley, garlic, salt and olive oil in a blender and blend for 1 minute until smooth.
4 Pour the pesto over the pasta and toss well. Serve warm.

STORAGE: Refrigerate the pesto for up to 3 days or freeze for up to 3 months.

095 Corn Pasta with Tomato Sauce

Corn pasta adds a different grain to your pasta options. This recipe makes more tomato sauce than you will need for the pasta, but it's great to have to hand for quick meals.

SERVES: 2 adults and 2 children   **PREP TIME:** 20 mins   **COOK TIME:** 1¼ hours

Tomato Sauce:
2 tbsp extra virgin olive oil
2 large onions, chopped
1 red pepper, deseeded and chopped
4 garlic cloves, chopped
3 bay leaves
2 tbsp chopped parsley
½ tsp dried thyme
1 tsp dried oregano

1 tsp dried basil
½ tsp fine sea salt
650g/1lb 7oz tomatoes, chopped
455ml/16fl oz/scant 2 cups passata
85g/3oz tomato purée

Pasta:
300g/10½oz dried corn spirelli
fine sea salt

1 To make the tomato sauce, heat the olive oil in a large saucepan over a medium-high heat. Add the onions and cook for 10 minutes, stirring occasionally, until brown. Add the pepper and cook, stirring, for a further 5 minutes, then stir in the remaining ingredients. Bring the mixture to the boil, then reduce the heat to low and simmer, covered, for 1 hour, stirring occasionally.

2 When the sauce has finished cooking, bring a small saucepan of salted water to the boil over a high heat and cook the pasta according to the packet instructions.

3 Drain the pasta, then return it to the pan. Add 185ml/6fl oz/¾ cup of the tomato sauce and mix well. Serve hot.

STORAGE: Refrigerate the sauce for up to 3 days or freeze in portion-sized jars for up to 3 months.

096 **Sweet Potato & Carrot Patties**

These delicious patties are always a hit at playdates and parties, or as a starter. You can make them ahead of time and keep them warm in the oven.

SERVES: 2 adults and 2 children   **PREP TIME:** 15 mins   **COOK TIME:** 30 mins

450g/1lb sweet potatoes, diced
225g/8oz carrots, thinly sliced
1 tbsp sesame seeds
3–4 spring onions, sliced

wholemeal spelt or wheat flour, as needed
4 tbsp Greek yogurt
½ tsp curry powder
sliced cucumber, to serve

1 Put the sweet potatoes and carrots in a steamer and steam, covered, over boiling water for 20 minutes until soft. Meanwhile, put the sesame seeds in a medium saucepan and heat over a medium-low heat for 3–4 minutes, shaking the pan occasionally, until the seeds begin to brown and just start popping. Set aside.

2 Preheat the grill to medium. Put the sweet potatoes and carrots in a bowl and mash with a fork, then mix in the sesame seeds and spring onions. Shape the mixture into 12 balls of equal size, then flatten into 6cm/2½in patties about 2cm/¾in high. If they are very sticky, sprinkle both sides with flour. Put on a baking sheet and grill for 5 minutes on each side until warmed through and lightly browned.

3 Meanwhile, put the yogurt and curry powder in a small bowl and mix well. Serve the patties warm with the sauce and sliced cucumber.

STORAGE: Refrigerate the patty mixture for up to 3 days.

HEALTH BENEFITS

SWEET POTATO is a great source of beta-carotene, which helps to raise blood levels of vitamin A, promoting your child's growth.

CUCUMBER provides silica, which helps to strengthen connective tissue. It also contains folate and vitamins A and C.

097 Cheesy Polenta Bites

Your little one will go back for more and more of this simply irresistible finger food – kids love the delicious melted cheese. These are great as part of a meal or as an afternoon snack.

SERVES: 2 adults and 2 children   **PREP TIME:** 10 mins   **COOK TIME:** 20 mins

butter, for greasing
1¼ tsp fine sea salt
150g/5½oz/1 cup polenta

75g/2½oz Parmesan cheese,
   coarsely grated
25g/1oz Parmesan cheese, finely grated

1 Preheat the grill to medium and grease the bottom of a 26cm/10½in square baking tin with butter. In a heavy-based saucepan, bring 750ml/26fl oz/3 cups water to the boil over a high heat. Add the salt and then the polenta, whisking vigorously to avoid lumps before it begins to thicken. Reduce the heat to medium-low and cook for 15 minutes, stirring continuously with a wooden spoon, until thick and stiff. Remove from the heat, then mix in the coarsely grated Parmesan cheese.

2 Pour the polenta into the prepared baking tin. Smooth out the surface using a rubber spatula. Spread from the centre outwards, pushing the polenta into the corners. Sprinkle the finely grated Parmesan over.

3 Grill for 5 minutes until lightly browned. Leave to cool for 10 minutes until set. Cut into 2.5cm/1in squares and serve hot, warm or cold.

STORAGE: Refrigerate for up to 3 days.

098 Tofu Squares

Herbivores and carnivores alike will love these highly flavoured, bite-sized squares of tofu. Tofu absorbs the flavours it's cooked with, and the tamari and garlic here really add pizzazz. Serve this with a pasta or rice dish and steamed veggies.

SERVES: 2 adults and 2 children   **PREP TIME:** 10 mins, plus 1 hour marinating   **COOK TIME:** 10 mins

4 tbsp tamari

2 garlic cloves, finely chopped

375g/13oz firm tofu,
   cut into 24 cubes of equal size

2 tsp toasted sesame oil

1 Put the tamari and garlic in a large, shallow dish. Add the tofu and then turn each piece over to coat in the marinade. Cover and chill for 1 hour or overnight.

2 Heat the sesame oil in a large frying pan over a medium-high heat. When it is hot, add the tofu and marinade. Cook for 5 minutes on each side, carefully turning the tofu squares over one by one until they are browned, the liquid has evaporated and the garlic is lightly fried. Serve hot or warm.

STORAGE: Refrigerate for up to 3 days

099 Cream Cheese & Salmon Blinis

These make a lovely meal, but they're also perfect for parties. If everything is prepared in advance, these are easy to assemble on the big day.

SERVES: 2 adults and 2 children   **PREP TIME:** 15 mins   **COOK TIME:** 20 mins

40g/1½oz/¼ cup buckwheat flour
30g/1oz/¼ cup wholemeal spelt
   or wheat flour
½ tsp baking powder
⅛ tsp fine sea salt

1 egg
55g/2oz/¼ cup cream cheese
100g/3½oz smoked salmon,
   cut into bite-sized pieces

1 Put the buckwheat flour, spelt flour, baking powder and salt in a medium bowl and mix well. Add the egg and 5 tablespoons water and whisk for 1–2 minutes until blended.

2 Heat a griddle over a medium-low heat. When it is hot, drop teaspoonfuls of the batter onto the griddle, spacing them well apart as they will spread into 6cm/2½in-wide circles. If the mixture is too thick and the blinis don't spread, add a little more water. Cook for 2–3 minutes until bubbles have popped on the surface and the undersides of the blinis are lightly brown. Turn them over and cook for a further 2–3 minutes until lightly browned. Remove from the griddle and leave to cool.

3 Spread a little of the cream cheese on each blini, top with 1 piece of the salmon and serve.

STORAGE: The cooled blinis can be stored in an airtight container separated by layers of baking parchment. They will keep in the fridge for up to 3 days.

100 Sweet Potato Fish Balls

These unbelievably good fish balls are so quick to make, and they're a great way to get your child eating fish. You can also make these into larger fish cakes, if you like.

SERVES: 2 adults and 2 children   **PREP TIME:** 15 mins   **COOK TIME:** 25 mins

250g/9oz sweet potatoes, unpeeled
   and diced
225g/8oz skinned pollock or haddock fillet,
   roughly chopped (check for bones)

1 egg, beaten
¼ tsp fine sea salt

1 Put the sweet potatoes in a steamer and steam, covered, over boiling water for 10 minutes until beginning to soften. Add the fish and continue steaming for a further 5 minutes until the fish is just cooked and the sweet potato is soft.

2 Preheat the grill to medium-high. Transfer the sweet potato and fish to a bowl and roughly mash with a fork until the mixture comes together but is still chunky. Mix in the egg and salt. The mixture will be a little sticky. Using a large melon baller or two teaspoons, scoop portions of the mixture onto a baking sheet. Grill for 4–5 minutes on each side until lightly browned and heated through. Serve warm.

STORAGE: Refrigerate for up to 2 days.